Artists at Work

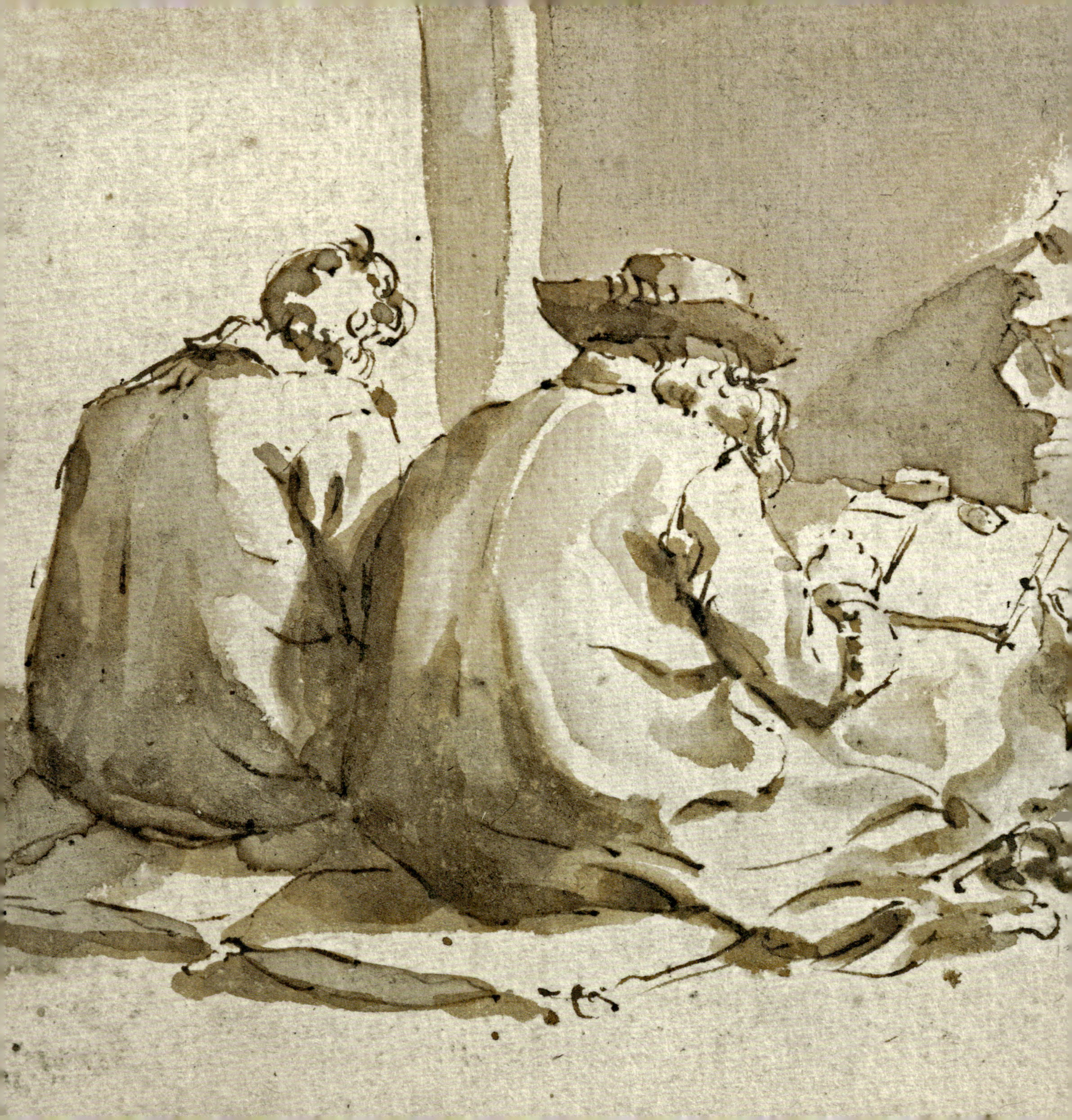

Artists at Work

Deanna Petherbridge and Anita Viola Sganzerla

EDITED BY

Ketty Gottardo and Rachel Sloan

THE COURTAULD Gallery

First published to accompany

Artists at Work

The Courtauld Gallery, London, 3 May – 15 July 2018

The Courtauld Gallery is supported by the
Higher Education Funding Council for England (HEFCE)

The programme of the Gilbert and Ildiko Butler Drawings Gallery is generously supported by
The International Music and Art Foundation

ISBN 978-1-911300-44-1

British Library Cataloguing in Publication Data

A catalogue record for this book is available from the British Library

Produced by Paul Holberton Publishing
89 Borough High Street, London SE1 1NL
WWW.PAULHOLBERTON.COM

Designed by Laura Parker

Printing by Gomer Press, Llandysul

FRONT COVER: Cat. 19 (detail)
BACK COVER: Cat. 7 (detail)
FRONTISPIECE: Cat. 3 (detail, larger than actual size)

Contents

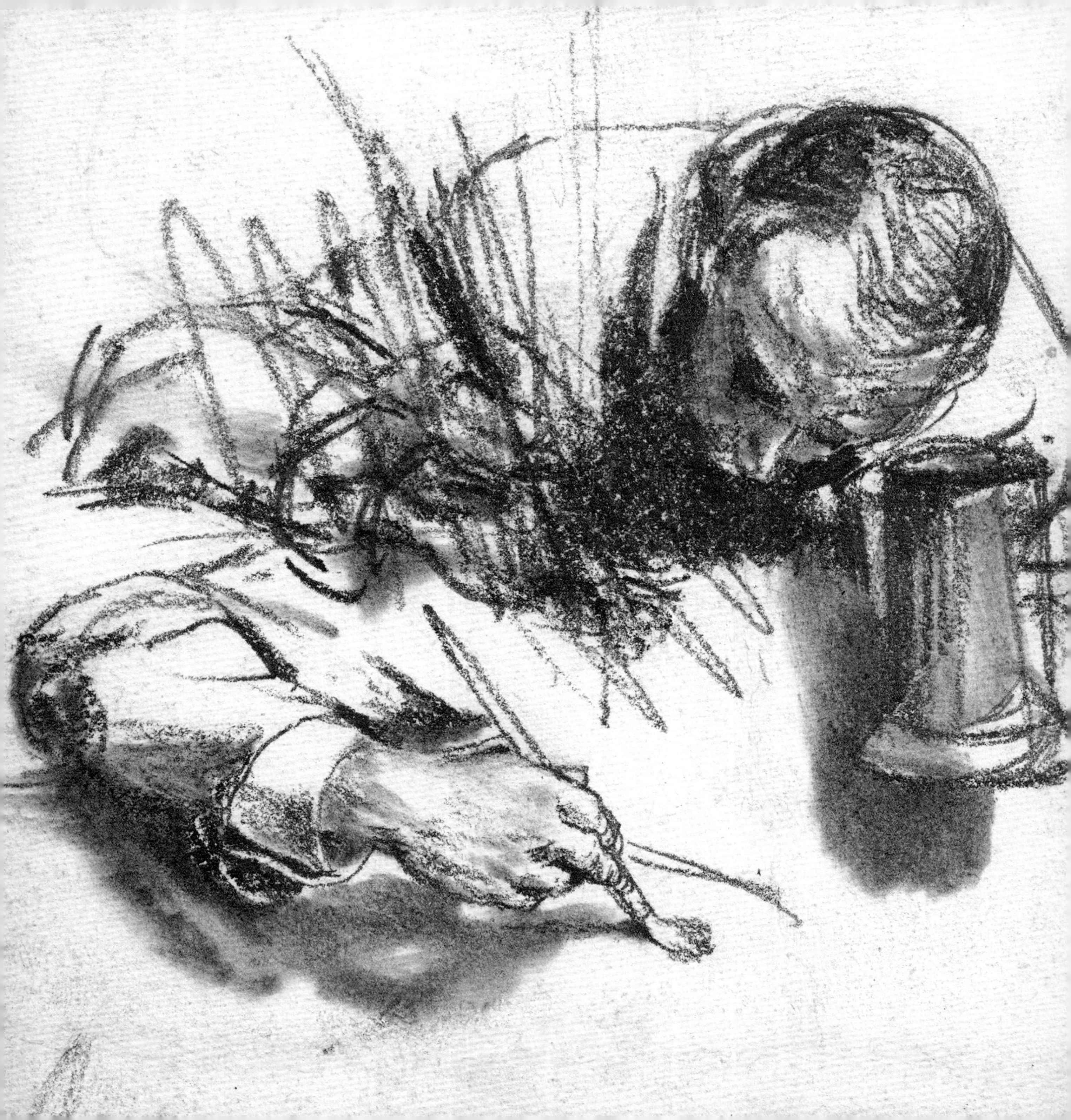

Foreword

Following *A Civic Utopia*, organised in 2016 with Drawing Matter Trust, *Artists at Work* is the second exhibition in the Gilbert and Ildiko Butler Drawings Gallery to present works chiefly from a single collection, other than The Courtauld's own, selected and interpreted by a distinguished guest curator. The collection in question has been assembled over many years with great care, knowledge and discernment. In its individuality, that is to say, its characterful thematic focus, pursued with flair and quality across a wide chronological range, it exemplifies the unique virtues of a private collection. We are immensely grateful to Katrin Bellinger for this fruitful and entirely enjoyable collaboration.

We are honoured that Deanna Petherbridge CBE, artist and writer, accepted the invitation to develop and curate this exhibition. Deanna Petherbridge has published, taught and lectured widely on drawing; her magnificent 2010 study, *The Primacy of Drawing: Histories and Theories of Practice*, stands as one of the most inspiringly original books on the subject. Deanna's own drawing-based practice gives the theme of this exhibition additional texture, and her spirited selection of works is characteristically open and thought-provoking.

I wish to extend my warm thanks to Anita Viola Sganzerla, curator of the Katrin Bellinger collection, who wrote the catalogue entries for this publication and contributed to many other aspects of the exhibition. Thanks are also due to Livia Schaafsma for her support. At The Courtauld Gallery I am delighted to acknowledge the contributions of Ketty Gottardo, our Martin Halusa Curator of Drawings, as well as Rachel Sloan, Rachel Hapoienu, Kate Edmondson, Julia Blanks and Chloe Le Tissier. For the generous loan of a riveting drawing by Cornelis Dusart we are indebted to the peerless Department of Prints and Drawings of the British Museum. The Tavolozza Foundation has kindly supported photography for the catalogue, as well as mounting and reframing. Finally, I have the pleasure of thanking the International Music and Art Foundation for its generous support of the varied and ambitious programme in the Butler Drawings Gallery. The Foundation has been critical in making drawings a central part of The Courtauld's public mission.

ERNST VEGELIN VAN CLAERBERGEN
Head of The Courtauld Gallery

Detail of cat. 13

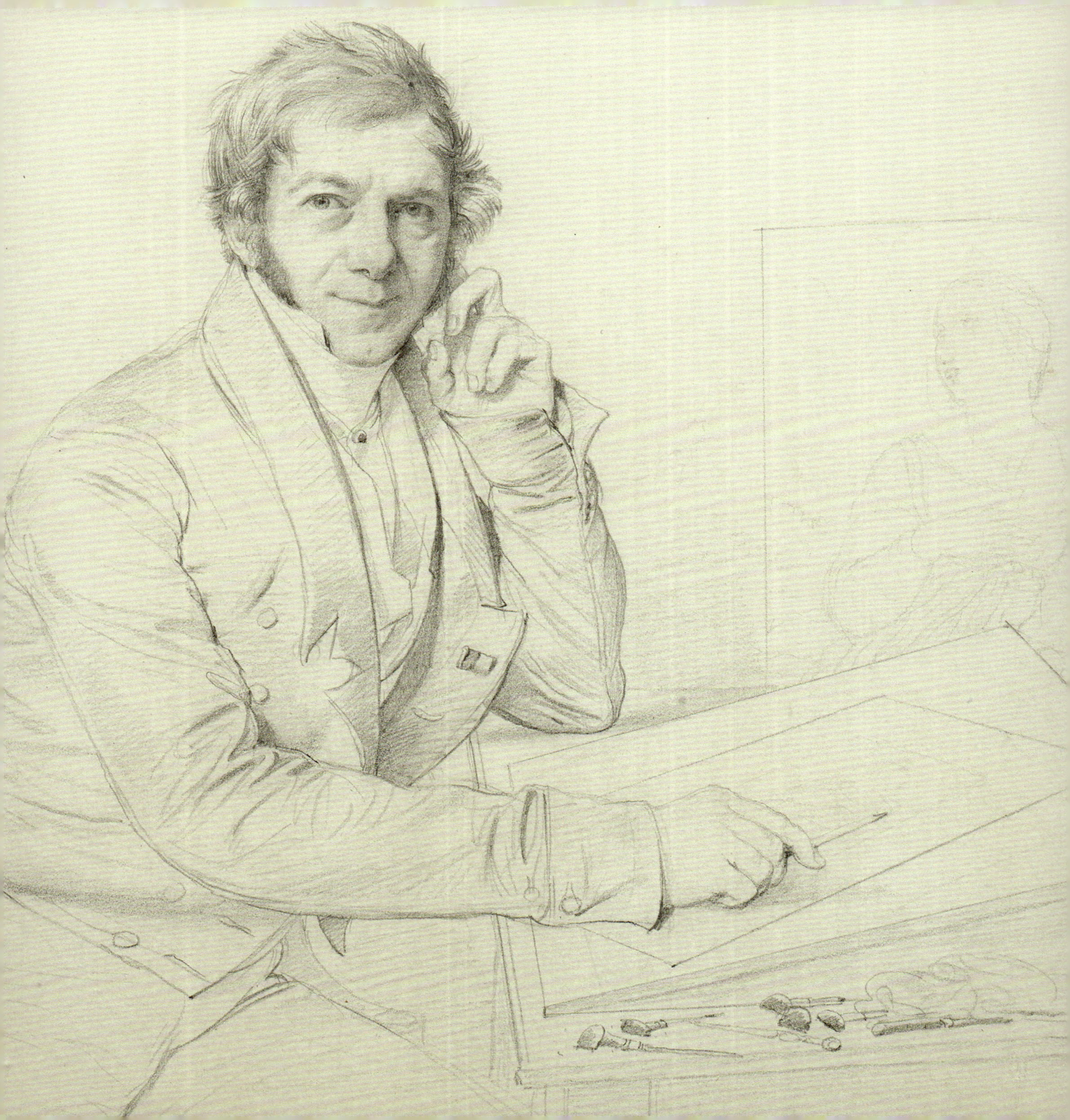

Preface

My collection focuses on drawings, paintings, prints, sculpture and photographs that depict artists at work, ranging from early book illuminations to contemporary art. I have been fascinated by this subject since I was young, when I unsuccessfully attempted to be an artist. It was when copying Old Master drawings during my time at art school that I acknowledged my limited talent but discovered the world of works on paper.

This led me to a career as a dealer in Old Master drawings, during which I started collecting, driven by the desire to keep some works for myself. Over thirty years later, now that I am no longer dealing, the collection has grown to more than a thousand pieces, and it gives me great satisfaction every day. I still enjoy taking that look over artists' shoulders, into their studios, observing their practice, depicted with such variety that I never tire of the theme.

One of the great pleasures of collecting is showing the works to others who are equally interested, and hearing their thoughts. Over the years many artists have viewed my collection and I have found their responses are often quite different from those of connoisseurs or art historians, for what they bring is a knowledge and approach informed by their own practice.

I was therefore delighted when Deanna Petherbridge came to visit. Herself an artist and draughtswoman, she has also written extensively about the subject of the artist at work. In her great publication *The Primacy of Drawing*, two chapters are dedicated to depictions of artists in drawings. I had always been impressed with her observations on the subject and was delighted when my friend Niall Hobhouse introduced us. The introduction resulted in my visit to her studio, where I much enjoyed looking at her drawings, and she in turn came to see my collection. Many works were like old friends to Deanna because she had come across images of them but did not know they were owned by me. After making her way through many boxes filled with drawings, prints and photographs as well as framed works, she suggested that she would love to curate an exhibition from my holdings. We both agreed that The Courtauld's Drawings Gallery would be an ideal space to exhibit the small, focused selection she would make.

It has been an all-round pleasurable experience to work on this show, guided by Deanna's vision, along with the great support the idea immediately received from Ketty Gottardo and Ernst Vegelin van Claerbergen at The Courtauld, and the hard work writing and researching the catalogue Anita Viola Sganzerla has put in, helped by Livia Schaafsma.

I hope you will enjoy the result of this fruitful cooperation.

KATRIN BELLINGER

Detail of cat. 15

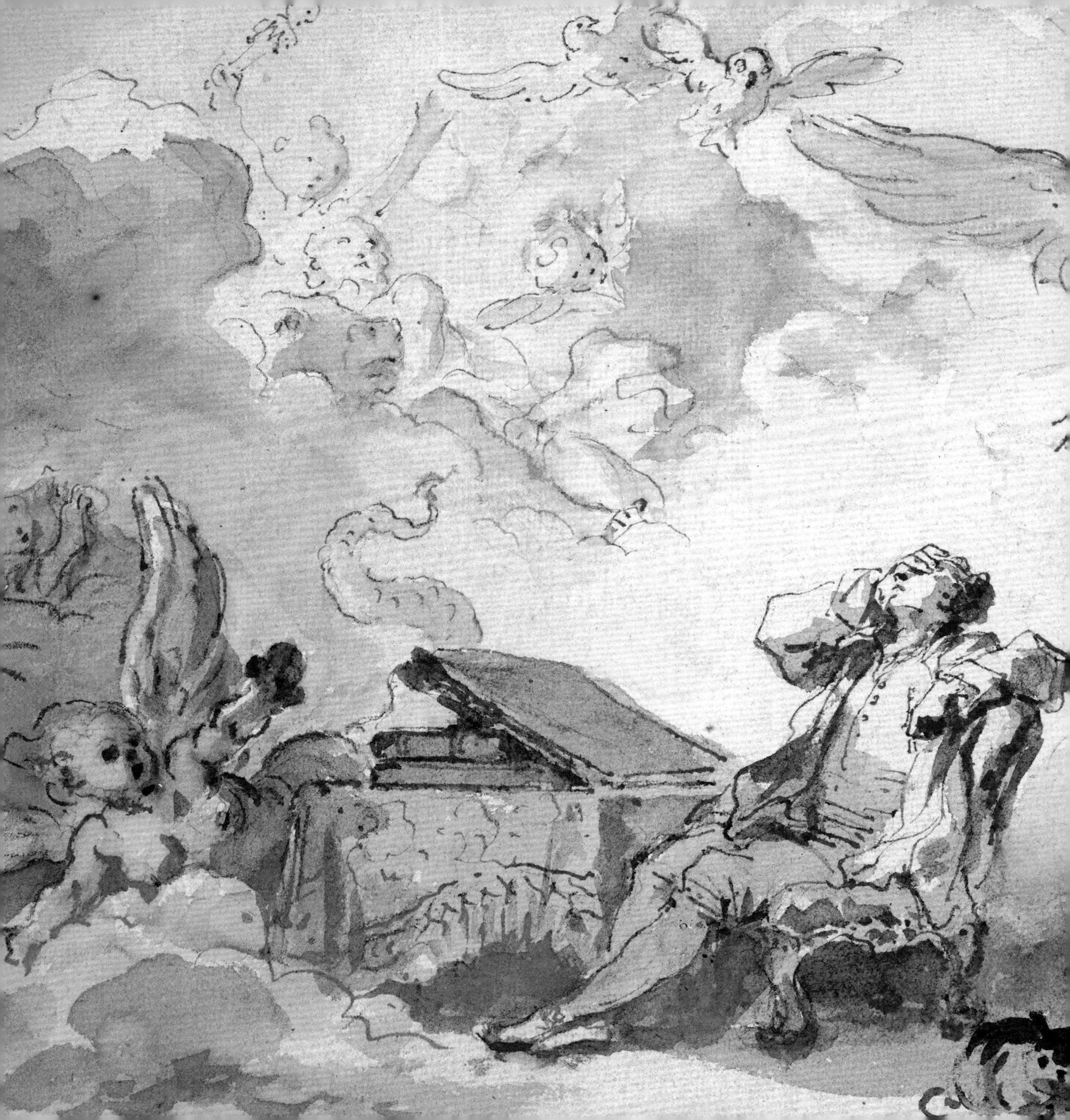

Playful Images of Allegory and Actuality

DEANNA PETHERBRIDGE

Artists at work is a rich and expansive topic that embraces history and contemporaneity, encompasses the sublime and the everyday, the solemn set-piece and the ridiculous moment, the distinguished artist and the amateur, through grand finished drawings to throw-away sketches. All of these are represented in the very fine specialist collection of Katrin Bellinger, from which the majority of drawings in this exhibition have been selected.

When students find themselves drawing their fellow pupils during a life class, or while laboriously copying from the antique amongst ruins or when recording the natural world in a sketchbook, this act has traditionally been interpreted as spontaneous and unselfconscious. Such drawings mark a shift away from perceptual practice, that is, the apparently direct and unmediated recording of the live model, antique sculpture or the landscape, to the conceptualisation of another viewer participating in the activity of art-making. So, although this reflexive practice has been designated as 'natural' by Western art theorists over many centuries, it is actually more distanced or even subversive than it might appear. For example, we can safely assume a degree of sophistication about vision as well as humour in an absolutely delightful small sketch by landscapist Henri-Joseph Harpignies (1819–1916) where an intrepid, behatted artist takes to a tree with his entire box of painting tricks to record the riverine scene below (fig. 1). Small figures carrying painting equipment often wander into the monochrome brush-and-wash sketches of Harpignies's late career, although they are not present in his many varieties of formal painted landscapes of France or Italy. In another charming drawing by him in the Bellinger collection, two practitioners crouched over their sketchbooks immerse themselves in a grey-washed dappled Arcadia, one well hemmed in visually by the very steep hillock on which the other is improbably perched. The exaggeration of this sketching knoll is amusing in a teacher who advised his pupils, "Examine nature under all conditions and love it like a mistress ... and above all never be unfaithful to it".[1]

Art history has taught us a proper wariness of the variant ideologies clustering around the generalised concepts of 'nature' and 'realism', so it would be naive *not* to question the supposedly quotidian pragmatism of sketches of other artists at work, self-portraits or studio views. The ubiquity and misleading modesty of these generic themes are underpinned by something more profound than unreflective graphic gestures of wit, witness or ownership. Rather, they are a response to the persistent need of artists across the centuries to celebrate their profession by representing acts of invention, as well as the materials and paraphernalia of practice, as meaningful signifiers of creativity.[2] This comment does not rest on faux re-readings of history to fit modern psychoanalytical notions about creativity. Artists' studios, workshops and academies have always been represented, even when invention and execution attracted different theoretical justifications

Detail of cat. 20

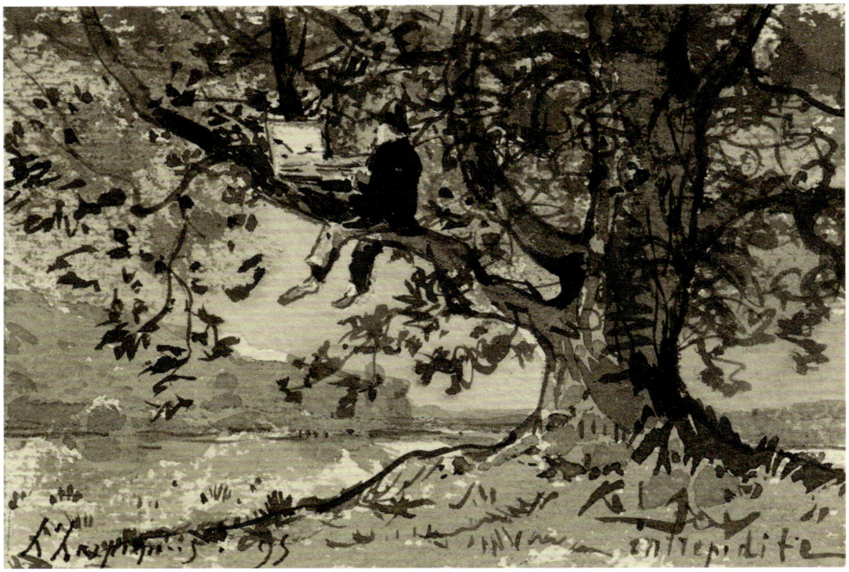

FIG. 1
Henri-Joseph Harpignies (1819–1916),
A draughtsman sketching, seated on a branch of a tree, pen and black ink, grey wash, over traces of chalk, 68 × 102 mm, Katrin Bellinger collection, inv. no. 2013-016

and were regarded as separate functions.[3] In this century, the professionalism of *making* art and the strategies and materials of practice have been re-evaluated by art historians – all the more so in drawing, where the potency of practice rests in its contingency and suggestibility as first-thought sketch, *primo pensiero,* as well as in all the complex factors that cluster around *dessein/disegno* as a learned practice related to works in other media. The transformative potential of the drawing and the act of drawing are perpetually in a state of becoming, and valued for this reason.

The creative divine

... the epithet of divine [...] *may be said to preside, like a supreme judge, over all the productions of nature; appearing to be possessed of the will and intention of the Creator*
— Sir Joshua Reynolds, *Discourse* III, 14 December 1770[4]

The iconography of Saint Luke the Evangelist as healer and artist, represented in the act of drawing or painting the Virgin Mary from life, situates image-making at the very centre of the Christian mysteries, both Catholic and Orthodox.[5] In post-Iconoclastic Byzantium, Saint Luke was celebrated for having painted the Virgin as Mother of God holding the Christ Child (*Theotokos* or God-bearer) and as guide to salvation (*Hodigitria*). The associated legends record that the Evangelist Luke listened to Mary talking while he was painting her, only writing down her history of the Passion afterwards, thereby imparting primacy to the visual over textual witness.[6] The legendary Byzantine icon *Salus Populi Romani* (Protectress of the Roman people) arrived in Rome, courtesy of Saint Helena, who supposedly discovered it in Jerusalem (while another image went to Constantinople) and was installed in Santa Maria Maggiore under papal patronage. Other Italo-Byzantine images attributed to the hand of the Apostle attained a mystical status in Italy during the late Middle Ages.[7] In the eleventh century, the Paduan cult of Saint Luke was established and the later proliferation of Guilds of Saint Luke throughout Europe, embracing physicians, painters and sculptors as well as other trades, served to popularise the subject in illuminations and altarpieces.[8] Such images, exemplified by the Gothic masterpiece of *Saint Luke drawing the Virgin* (c.1435–40) by Rogier van der Weyden (c.1400–1464), extant in four versions from the period, were of particular significance during the fifteenth and sixteenth centuries in the Low Countries, where there was a Guild of Saint Luke in every major city.[9] Paintings of the patron saint of the artists' guild were commissioned by local guilds for chapels, gifted to guild halls, or were a popular subject for the masterwork required for guild matriculation.[10]

Art historians seldom discriminate between painting and drawing in the titles they have bestowed on images of Saint Luke portraying the Virgin, yet as the guilds developed they became more and more concerned with the 'arts of design'.[11] Two iconographical models for representing this theme developed in Catholic and Protestant Europe from the fifteenth century onwards. In one, the Evangelist and the holy Mother and Child inhabit the same architectural space as sentient beings, breathing the same air, so to speak, while he draws or paints her. In the other, the Virgin appears before Saint Luke the artist as an apparition floating in an insubstantial cloud or in an almond-shaped penumbra supported by angels.[12]

A very fine roundel drawing on grey prepared paper attributed to Jan de Beer, a member of the Antwerp Guild of Saint Luke, is believed to be a study for a stained-glass window for the guild's chapel (fig. 2). It relates compositionally to a painting of the same subject by de Beer now in Milan.[13] However the ox, wearing the guild's emblem of three shields around its neck, has been moved into a linking position between the Evangelist and the Mother of God in order to maximise the circular organisation of the drawn version. The haloed and enthroned Virgin in complicated robes supports the naked Christ Child on her lap, making a gesture of blessing. The Evangelist is painting at his easel, holding in his left hand a small palette and a mahl-stick, which is used as a support for his right hand, wielding the brush. Any number of architectural details and artistic paraphernalia are precisely delineated in the grand ecclesiastical arched studio, while a winged angel with sleeves rolled up grinds pigments at a table in a workshop area to the right.[14]

Despite this early example, the inclusion of (non-angelic) studio assistants grinding paint in the iconography of artists' studios is commonly attributed to the influence of Giorgio Vasari's interpretations of the lives of artists from the ancient world in Pliny the Elder's *Natural History*, Book XXXV.[15] Vasari's fresco of *Saint Luke painting the Virgin* (c.1567–72) in the Cappella di San Luca in Santissima Annunziata in Florence, a memorial chapel for artists associated with the Accademia del Disegno, was probably completed by Alessandro Allori (1535–1607). In the freely sketched but squared-up preparatory pen-and-ink drawing in the Prado (fig. 3), the fully rounded Virgin with the Christ Child in one arm floats on clouds supported by angelic putti. The bearded Evangelist seated on an elaborate stool at his square-topped easel wears classical dress and holds a very small palette. Three admiring attendants (only two appear in the fresco) crowd the working studio to the right of Saint Luke, while the almond-shaped aureole of the divine manifestation on the left is lit with a spectral glow indicated by radiating lines. A lightly sketched pigment grinder is at work in a room above the studio on the right, translated into a burly worker in the completed fresco in Florence.

A squared-up drawing by the Northern Mannerist artist Hendrick de Clerck, who was court painter to the Archdukes Ernest and, later, Albert and Isabella in Brussels, depicts a bearded Saint Luke leaning forward on his stool to draw the Virgin's face on a board in a pose of semi-genuflection (fig. 4). The haloed Virgin is engaged in entertaining a lively Christ Child, who points towards the carefully observing saint, who has sketched the Madonna's face on his tablet. They inhabit the same architectural space, which, apart from the flasks and objects on a draped

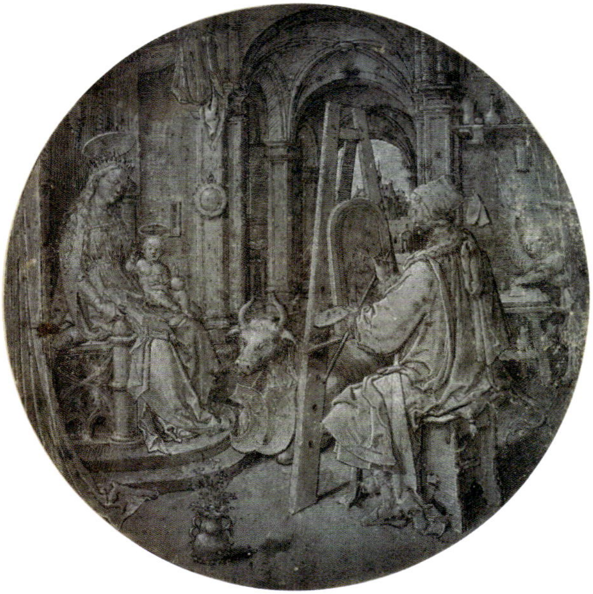

FIG. 2
Attributed to Jan de Beer (1475–1528), *Saint Luke painting the Virgin,* c.1509, brush and black ink, grey wash, heightened with white on grey prepared paper pricked for transfer, 289 mm diam., British Museum, London, inv. no. 1860,0616.57

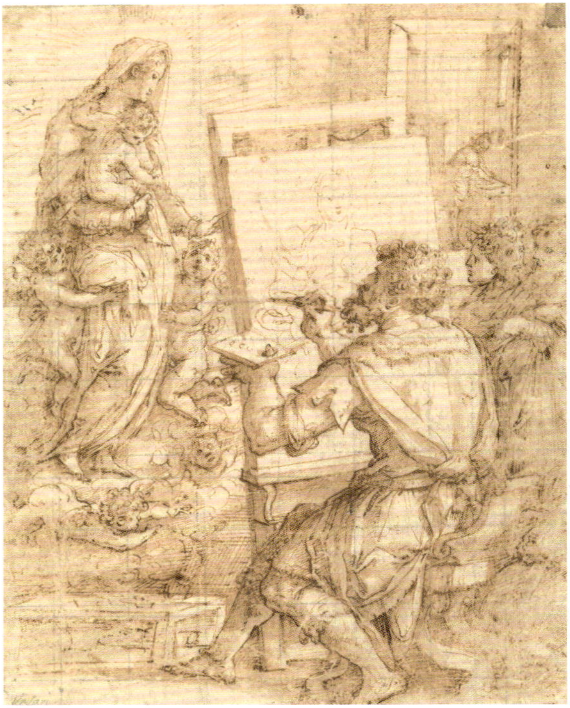

FIG. 3
Giorgio Vasari (1511–1574), *Saint Luke painting the Virgin*, c. 1567–72, black chalk and brown ink and wash, 264 × 214 mm, Museo Nacional del Prado, Madrid, inv. no. D01563

studio table, has the appearance of a Renaissance church. Rounded classical niches and high-set columns are set at an angle to an opening which shows an open landscape with hills beyond. The attendant ox imparts a certain down-to-earth note to the scene in front of this backdrop, but a cloud of winged putti angels and cherubim above the Virgin's canopy proclaim her divine status.

Genre details tend to become obscured in Baroque interpretations of this theme that transform the act of representation into an unearthly drama between the earth-bound Evangelist and the Virgin as a heavenly apparition. This is so in an intense drawing on blue paper, *Saint Luke drawing the Virgin*, by the Parma-born artist Giovanni Lanfranco (fig. 5).[16] The artist/Evangelist, in a twisted and dramatic pose, looks ecstatically upwards towards the floating Virgin and Child, swirling in indeterminate dark and light washes and cloud formations. Although he is grounded while she is floating on clouds, the entire interaction takes place within an inspirational space of other-worldliness. The only manifestations of human activities are the square palette and brushes lying on a sloping ground in front of the partly bare-legged Saint

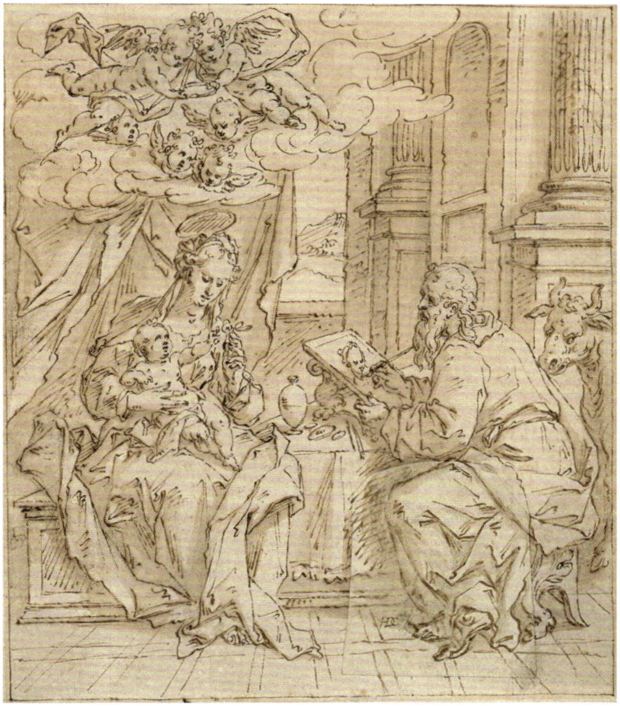

FIG. 4
Hendrick de Clerck (c.1560–1630), *Saint Luke drawing the Virgin*, pen and brown ink and wash, squared in black chalk, 290 × 253 mm, Katrin Bellinger collection, inv. no. 2010-006

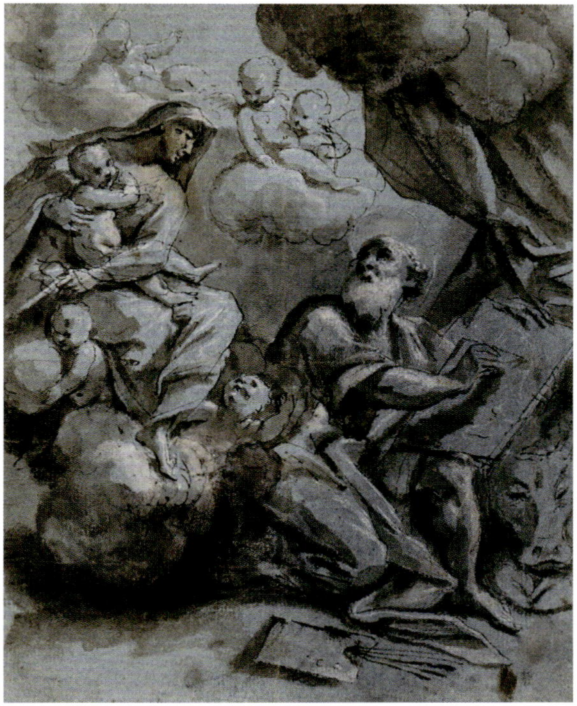

FIG. 5
Giovanni Lanfranco (1582–1647), *Saint Luke drawing the Virgin*, pen and brown ink with brown wash, heightened with white on blue paper, 251 × 198 mm, British Museum, London, inv. no. 1992,0516.108

Luke. Lanfranco painted another version of the subject in Naples, where he moved after a period as principal of the Accademia di San Luca in Rome.[17] This would be drawn and etched by Jean-Honoré Fragonard, as will be discussed below, indicating the fascination of later artists with this *topos* of divine artistic practice.

The 'divine' artist: genius, fame and envy

Designations of late medieval and early Renaissance famous men (*uomini famosi*) as divine, for example Dante Alighieri or the mathematician Luca Pacioli, relate to the classical precedents of so naming Homer and Plato.[18] In antiquity, visual arts were not firmly allied with the Liberal Arts, not even as defined by Pliny, who in the Renaissance was a key source of information on visual precedents. By the fifteenth century, however, 'divine' as a term of esteem and adulation was not uncommonly applied to the artists Mantegna, Fra Angelico, Perugino and the architect Brunelleschi. Vasari described Michelangelo's works as divine more than twenty times in the first, 1550 edition of his *Lives of the Artists*, rising to nearly forty instances in the edition of 1568.[19] The encomium *divino* relates to the

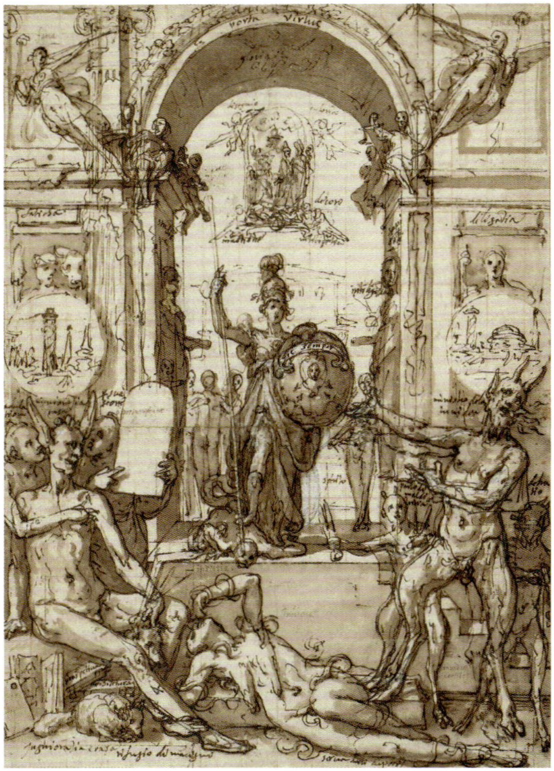

FIG. 6
Federico Zuccaro (c.1540/42–1609), *Porta Virtutis: Art triumphant over Ignorance and Calumny*, pen and brown wash, some corrections in white bodycolour, squared in red chalk, 378 × 276 mm, Christ Church, Oxford, inv. no. 0213

possession of *ingegno*, translated into English variously as 'creative invention' or 'genius'.[20] Federico Zuccaro, who completed Vasari's frescoes in the dome of Florence Cathedral, notoriously played word-games with the term *disegno*, suggesting it was the '*segno di dio*' (sign of God) in his treatise on artistic 'idea' or intellectual inspiration. Zuccaro, who was involved with the establishment of the Accademia del Disegno in Florence in 1563 and of the Accademia di San Luca in Rome in 1593–94, suggested a tripart division of *disegno interno* (as opposed to *disegno esterno*) into the categories *divino*, *angelico* and *umano*.[21]

This is not the place for an excursus into Renaissance art theory, except to emphasise that creating art is always imbued with aspects of the numinous as well as the pragmatic, whatever the doctrinal means with which it is constructed and justified. The flip side of fame and genius, however, is the envy of other artists.[22] Classical precedents are found in Pliny's anecdote of Ptolemy's jester, whom jealous rivals had suborned to invite Apelles falsely to the king's banquet, and in Lucian's description of the *Calumny of Apelles*, recreated in paintings by Botticelli and Federico Zuccaro.[23] The subject was of personal interest to the fiery Zuccaro, who was expelled from Rome in October 1581 by the Bolognese-born Pope Gregory XIII for temporarily displaying a satirical artwork on the façade of the church of San Luca on the saint's feast day.[24] Zuccaro's riposte to the expulsion order was the drawing *Porta Virtutis: Art triumphant over Ignorance and Calumny* (1581; fig. 6).[25] An armed Minerva is framed in the triumphal arch of Virtue, her foot crushing the figure of Calumny, with a number of allegorical personages arranged in the frontal space in dramatic poses. Written inscriptions in the artist's hand inform us which are the artistic virtues (including *disegnio, colorito, invention, faticha*), and which are malign personages. Crass ignorance (*ignorantia crasa*) in the left foreground is listening to Adulation (*adulatione*) with her arms around nude Persuasion (*persuatione*), identified by his long asses' ears. Aged Envy (*invidia*), wreathed with snakes, writhes in the centre, eating her heart out in all the un-voluptuous horror of her long skinny breasts, while the group on the right entitled *ministro della invidia* includes a bearded and ithyphallic satyr pointing to the action like a showman at a fair.[26]

Both Virtue and Envy are called upon in a puzzling small drawing, *Virtue protecting the Artist* (1587; cat. 22), attributed to the German artist David Kandel. The armed female personification of Virtue in swirling drapery is winged and

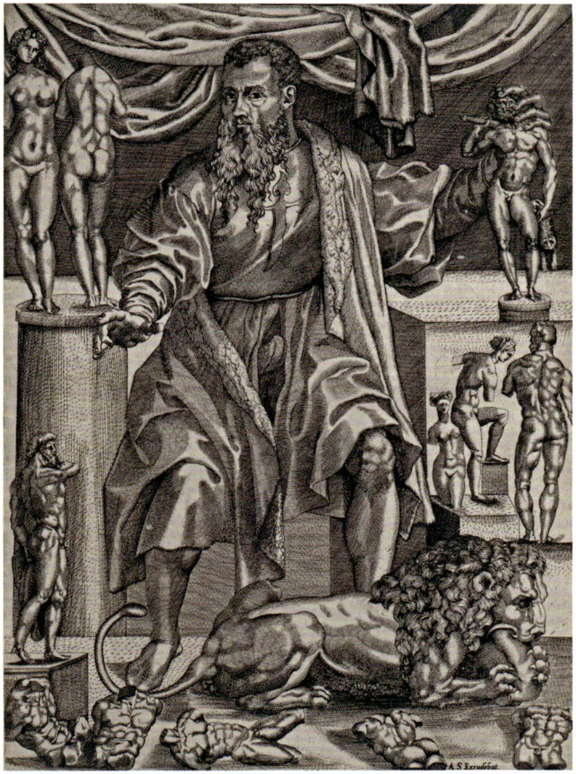

FIG. 7
Anonymous 16th-century artist after Niccolò della Casa (fl.1543–48) after Baccio Bandinelli (1493–1560), *Self-portrait of Baccio Bandinelli*, 1548, engraving, 416 × 306 mm, Katrin Bellinger collection, inv. no. 2003-020

bare-breasted; she holds a palm branch in her right hand and a laurel wreath in her hair. Her very large shield is held out to protect the drawing artist from the lightning and hailstones of envy.[27] Pliny's adage *nulla dies sine linea*, encouraging artists not to pass a day without drawing practice, is probably the virtuous activity promoted here. The classically dressed young artist is so concentrated on the drawing held on a board on one bent knee that he does not even look up at this symbolic intervention. The small statuette on the plinth in front of him, a studio model of the type of the Cnidian Venus holding her drapery in front of her, appears improbably to bend her (restored) head upwards to the threatening forces above!

The sculptor Baccio Bandinelli was renowned for his intense rivalry with Michelangelo. He is represented as a virile, bearded and dynamic genius artist surrounded by his own maquettes and classical remains in a version of a well-known print after his self-portrait (fig. 7). The stylised engraving techniques of narrow bands of contour shading and dotted cross-and-triple hatching contrasting with bright areas of paper acting as highlights serve to exaggerate the three-dimensionality of the muscular sculptures and drapery. Bandinelli's wide-spread legs rest in both Renaissance camps, classical antiquity and the politico-religious world of the cross of Saint James emblazoned on his chest.[28] Along with the date, the publisher has inscribed the print bottom right as *A.S. Excudebat*, employing the active voice of the Latin *excudere* (in this context meaning to print or to publish). This was not an uncommon practice in print publishing of the time in Italy and northern Europe, and links in – whether by chance or not – with Bandinelli's own self-conscious usage of what has been dubbed the 'Plinian signature'. This form was used in emulation of Michelangelo's deliberate carving of *faciebat* (the imperfect tense roughly translates as 'was making') into the marble band across the Virgin's chest in the *Pietà* (1496–98, Saint Peter's, Rome).[29] The choice of this tense of the verb *facere* (to make) 'introduced the conceit that the artist had not finished his creation ...and proclaimed the erudition and cultivation [of both artist and patron]'.[30]

Valued notions of unfinish and provisionality are radically associated with *disegno* in all its aspects, not just the *primo pensiero* sketch charged with invention. Drawings of artists at work assembled in this exhibition therefore share in this celebration of practice as an *ongoing and continuous activity,* not a sealed finality.

Allegories of the mythical studio

Apelles's dedication to drawing that inspired the proverb *nulla dies sine linea* occurs in Pliny's brief passage about Apelles's relationship with his patron Alexander the Great. Hiding in his studio, Apelles would secretly listen to the views of passers-by but objected to the shoemaker who criticised his work once too often: 'Let the cobbler stick to his last' (*ne sutor ultra crepidam*).[31] Alexander the Great was a frequent visitor to Apelles's studio, having issued an edict preventing any other artist from portraying his noble presence. However, when Alexander expressed too many opinions about art without sufficient knowledge, Apelles 'would politely advise him to drop the subject', suggesting that the studio apprentices engaged in grinding colours were laughing at his ignorance.[32] In spite of this put-down, Alexander conferred his favourite mistress Campaspe on the besotted Apelles, attesting to the esteem in which he held the artist. The subject was popularly set as a theme for artists' entrance pieces for the various Guilds of Saint Luke during the sixteenth and seventeenth centuries and became a standard competition narrative for European royal academies in the eighteenth century. Many of these drawn studies have been preserved in academies and often deploy an elaborate bed in deliberately erotic settings.[33]

The wonderful drawing of *Punchinello as portrait painter* by Giovanni Domenico Tiepolo from his late series *Divertimento per li regazzi* (Entertainments for children) is one of the star pieces of this exhibition (cat. 19). I believe that this beguiling drawing plays wittily with classical themes and theatrical encounters, transforming the theme of *Alexander the Great in the studio of Apelles,* painted three times by Domenico's father Giovanni Battista Tiepolo (1696–1770), into a *commedia dell'arte* masquerade. The masked Alexander the Great standing in the centre of the composition, with one arm casually resting on his hip, makes the well-established gesture of ceding Campaspe to Punchinello/Apelles, who is seated at the easel with brush and palette in hand. The artist sports the same leering mask and the tapering inquisition cap worn by all the other Punchinello players. Campaspe, with her everyday hat and folded fan, is fully dressed like the other women in the crowd, and she leans back in a chair in a worldly manner accompanied by the small Maltese pug dog that appears in Giovanni Battista's grandiose – and very different – oil painting of the same subject (c.1725–26, Museum of Fine Arts, Montreal). In Domenico's farcical drawn version, the villainous mountebanks crowded on the bare stage all look towards the gesturing and effete Alexander. Areas of paper left untouched by sepia wash as highlights are so boldly controlled that the oval frame on Punchinello's easel appears to throw a bright reflection on the corner of the room between the emperor and his mistress. It might be a mirror reflecting the artist-as-buffoon. In the foreground, balancing the highlighted principal figures, are two shadowy assistants grinding pigments on a stand.

The elements of this story – the male encounter with submissive female nudity as a spark to performative genius, which elevates the creative artist to a plane higher than military might and political power – lingers powerfully in representations of artists' studios even in the twentieth century. Picasso, for example, returned to the theme again and again in his sketchbooks. This *topos* is the profane shadow version of the saintly religious messenger painting the divinity of the Virgin Mary, and when artists meld together the sacred and profane by freely transposing iconographical elements from one narrative into another they proclaim a very wide entitlement for the transformative power of visual art.

For example, a rather formal and affectless black-chalk drawing of *Saint Luke painting the Virgin* by Charles-Nicolas Cochin the Younger, the French engraver, academician and art critic, depicts a mother and child seated at ground level alongside the artist at his easel as if they were mundane studio models (fig. 8). Cochin, who draws in a deliberately anti-Rococo manner, effects an extraordinary transposition of the pragmatic and the numinous. The canvas before

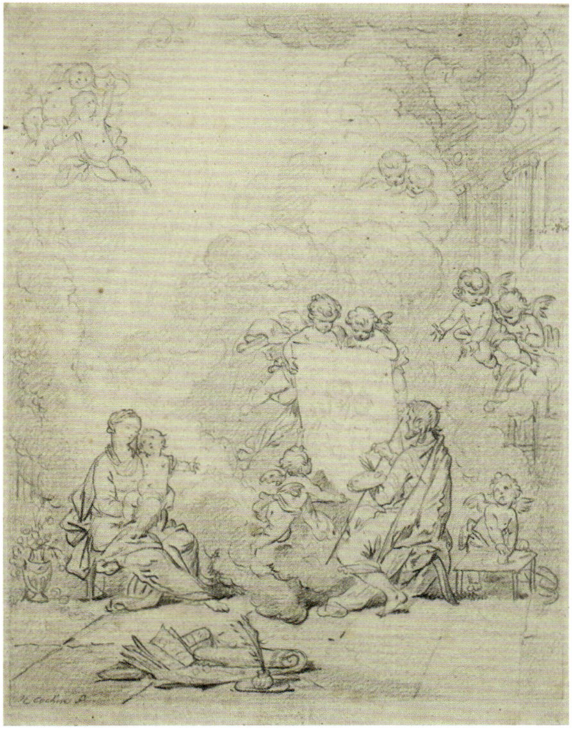

FIG. 8
Charles-Nicolas Cochin the Younger (1715–1790), *Saint Luke painting the Virgin*, black chalk, 213 × 172 mm, Katrin Bellinger collection, inv. no. 1996-004

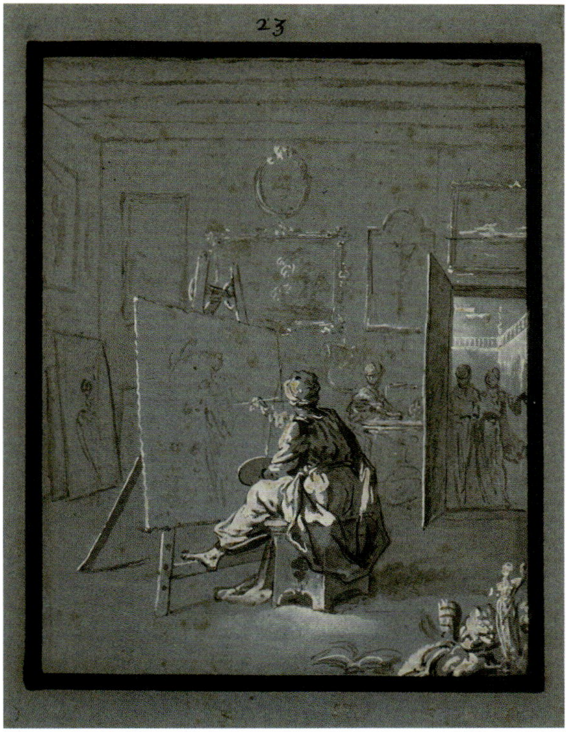

FIG. 9
Jean-Baptiste Oudry (1686–1755), *Artist at an easel*, pen and brown ink, brown wash, heightened with white on blue paper, 325 × 265 mm, Katrin Bellinger collection, inv. no. 2007-025

which the cloaked and bearded Evangelist is seated, armed with his extremely lengthy mahl-stick and palette, is the focus of the brightest areas of empty paper. The emphasis is therefore on the artwork-in-process, rather than the Virgin with Christ Child, who have none of the appurtenances of sacred figures. A collection of drawing and painting tools placed in the foreground form a cartouche in an exaggerated scale in relation to the protagonists of the scene.

It has recently been suggested that the drawing by Cochin's older colleague Jean-Baptiste Oudry of an *Artist at an easel* (fig. 9) is probably an image of Saint Lazarus Zographos of Constantinople, who was imprisoned and tortured by the iconoclastic Emperor Theophilus of the Eastern Roman (Byzantine) Empire but continued to paint icons in his cell.[34] According to new scholarship, the number 23 at the top of the sheet conforms to the missing sheets and index from Oudry's Album 3, *The Lives of the Saints*.[35] The narratives concerning Saint Lazarus in Byzantine chronicles attribute his artistic abilities to acts of contemplation that were a gift from God; he later helped to restore icons after the death of the emperor.

This sheet, however, does not illustrate any dramatic moment in the *Life*, as in other historiographical scenes in the album, but depicts a turbaned artist at work in a palatial studio. The few dashes on the very large canvas appear to be a landscape, and a rapidly sketched assistant grinds pigments at a table next to the open door. Two indeterminate figures are approaching from outside, but are not threatening gaolers. Light falls on the profile shape and drapery of the seated artist, on the canvas on the easel and on the Rococo frames on the wall, and spills over on to the floor, picking up the edges of the artist's stool. In this very eighteenth-century courtly view, the studio is anything but a workplace, although a highlighted cartouche of studio objects in the lower right-hand corner acts as a framing device and adds scale in an informally decorative manner.

In 1751 Cochin had visited Venice, where he admired the free painterly quality of *The Vision of Saint Jerome* by the German Baroque painter Johann Liss (c.1595–1631), in the church of San Niccolò da Tolentino. This enthusiasm was shared by Jean-Honoré Fragonard, who produced a drawing and later an etching of the work.[36] Fragonard's records of ecstatic subjects by Italian Baroque masters also included a drawing of *Saint Luke surrounded by angels* (1638–46) in the Church of the Holy Apostles in Naples by Lanfranco, and he produced an etching of the subject with the Apostle gazing upwards ecstatically.[37]

These copies provide the context for Fragonard's magnificent painterly and evocative brush drawing *The inspiration of the artist* (cat. 20), thought to be an allegorical self-portrait from the early 1760s. The dramatic pose of the central figure with his hand clapped to his thrown-back brow could, however, be a gesture of despair rather than exaltation, as the propped-up portfolio on the table is closed, suggesting creative block. The floating putti, winged angels, night birds and hybrid *chimerae* of the artist's imagination swirling around the central space are deliberately vague and lightly drawn, although a flying ox emerging from the clouds suggests the companion symbol of Saint Luke. A more intensely inked winged and dragon-tailed female harpy curls around the carpeted table as an evil genie. The drawing brings to mind the later well-known print by Francisco de Goya (1746–1828), *The sleep of reason produces monsters*, published as Plate 43 of *Los Caprichos* (c.1797–98). The huge lynx-like cat to the right of the dreamer is usually interpreted as symbolising visual acuity and reason, but Goya often included cats, owls, bats and harpies in the many witch-themed prints of the *Los Caprichos* cycle.

Inspiration or *enthusiasme* were long proposed by previous generations of scholars to be the spark behind Fragonard's bravura 'Fantasy figures' (*Figures de fantaisie*), paintings of artists and poets, revealed to the spectator through the 'natural' sign of the artist's agitated touch.[38] However, new scholarship based on a recently discovered sketch (c.1769) by Fragonard has led art historians firmly to associate these portraits with named individuals,[39] away from Mary Sheriff's earlier argument that 'they are marked by a display of creative prowess so insistent that the artist's self-presentation virtually eclipses his depiction of the sitters'.[40] Of the series, a figure in travelling clothes with his head raised and turned is a portrait of the abbé de Saint-Non (Jean-Claude Richard), Fragonard's friend and patron.[41] He travelled with Fragonard in Italy in 1761 and commissioned the artist to make copy drawings, subsequently publishing many of them as prints.[42] Fragonard might have been a secular artist of his time with totally different preoccupations, but he was willing to adapt and develop the visual rhetoric of divinely inspired invention from the Baroque era.[43]

The working studio: paint and performance

There would appear to be a huge distance between the mythical atelier that can accommodate emperors, angels and holy apparitions and the workaday artist's studio of hard grind and dirty brushes. But as the accoutrements of the studio – the easels, palettes, mahl-sticks and drawing implements – have been appropriated unchanged for allegorical themes, as discussed above, it is not difficult for us to acknowledge that core symbolic content can be wrapped within seemingly 'straightforward' genre depictions.

Netherlandish artist Cornelis Dusart inherited the studio of his master Adriaen van Ostade (1610–1685) and, like him, often addressed the subject of artists working in their studios in graphic media or paint as a genre subject with emblematic overtones. Dusart's brown-and-grey wash drawing *The old painter* (cat. 21) is possibly an allegory about sight, as the aged, bearded artist bends to peer through his pebble glasses at the hidden painting on the easel.[44] It could also be an allegory of the arts (there is a violin thrown casually on a studio bench alongside the easel) or a commentary on the adage *ars longa, vita brevis* (art is long, life is short).[45] His archaising jacket and cap are not in tatters, and, in spite of the cramped working studio, this appears not to be a satirical play on the poor unsuccessful artist, also a popular theme of the time. The extreme concentration of the artist is underlined by the deliberate disposition of brown and grey wash and careful depictions of the tools, boxes, bottles and model body-parts disposed on the shelves, as in artists' manuals of the time. Controlled highlights illuminate the frontal activities of painting, while the twisting staircase and back walls are slightly more shadowy.

Two hundred years later, Otto Greiner indulged in humorous drawings and prints of himself and other artists at work. The German Symbolist printmaker, illustrator and pupil of Max Klinger (1857–1920) produced highly eroticised images of witchcraft and misogynistic devilry in mock-academic guise, similar to the works of the Munich Symbolist Franz von Stuck (1863–1928), but he also addressed wide subjects in his day-to-day illustration projects. Greiner's *Portrait of an artist asleep on a chair in the studio* (fig. 10), with its pencil inscriptions, belongs to this relaxed genre and could be interpreted as a caricatural riff on 'divine' inspiration and artistic dream worlds. The slumbering artist stretches out in front of his work-table, with a shining halo around his snoring head, using studio plinths for leg support. The oversize palette on the table resembles that held by Greiner in other amusing self-portraits and the blind has slipped down the huge studio window, allowing for a dramatic contrast between dark shadowy washes and white background paper acting as highlights on horizontal surfaces.

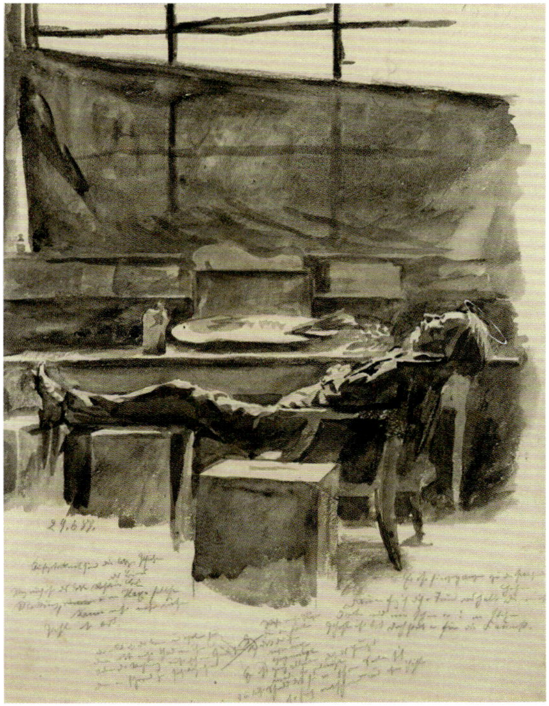

FIG. 10
Otto Greiner (1869–1916), *Portrait of an artist, asleep on a chair in the studio*, 1888, graphite and ink wash, 301 × 230 mm, Katrin Bellinger collection, inv. no. 2009-004

The Dalmatian-born artist Ermenegildo Antonio Donadini, who spent most of his life in Vienna and later Dresden as a royal portraitist, teacher, restorer and passionate photographer, was also a committed draughtsman. His very detailed drawings (and photographs) of elaborate nineteenth-century interiors include views of his own studios, for example *The artist's studio, Munich*, 1877 (cat. 11). A full-sized and dressed artist's mannequin is precariously collapsing on a box in this cluttered room in a historic building. In place of a head, a piece of wood bearing an elaborate beret emerges from the stuffing as the figure rests against a well-lit wall, filled with huge-scale trial sketches for a fresco. A small studio model of Jean-Antoine Houdon's *Ecorché* (1767) on a high shelf looms over the model's 'throne' with its eerie occupant. The studio is cluttered with exotic curiosities – stuffed birds, gourds, ceramics, costumes, carpets, musical instruments, swords, embroideries and pinned-up sketches. The relatively uninflected pencil lines of this complex interior add to the sense of the uncanny projected by the collapsing artist's dummy, awkwardly mysterious in its linear elaboration. The rhythms of this late nineteenth-century drawing are somehow Rococo, and it is appropriate that Donadini, as recorded in his autobiography, was later to paint a ceiling for the royal Villa Strehlen 'in the style of Tiepolo'.[46]

The equally long-lived but better-known German artist of an earlier generation, the printmaker and painter Adolph von Menzel (1815–1905), was also concerned with royal pomp and splendour – in his case, the neo-Rococo paintings and wood-engravings illustrating the life of the Prussian Frederick the Great (1712–1786) as well as scenes of everyday life in Berlin and Paris. The ambidextrous Menzel was frequently dubbed the Apelles of his time because of his unceasing devotion to drawing, which he recorded in innumerable series of pocket sketchbooks, drawn in later life with a carpenter's pencil using a finger as stump.[47] He was often quoted as saying, 'Every drawing is useful, and drawing everything is useful, too'.[48] The encyclopaedic range of this life project included sketches of people drawing, of objects in his studio and workmen in daily trades as well as industrial situations. The two views of a house painter at work, *Studies of a man painting* (cat. 13), appropriately capture the extreme concentration needed in wielding a brush, especially when assisted by a tankard of beer. This sketch relates to the house painters in Menzel's ironic gouache painting *Beati possidentes* (Happy owners; Georg Schäfer Museum, Schweinfurt), where the bourgeois owners congratulate themselves on their over-embellished mansion. However, Menzel's lightning-quick drawings from life have an entirely different flavour from his paintings, as he searches via *pentimenti* and rigorous crossings-out for the most telling position of arm to brush-hand to downward-turned head.

In 1866 Menzel visited the battlefields of the Austro-Prussian War, making moving drawings, sometimes in colour, of wounded soldiers and rotting military corpses. This experience was very far from the military circumstances of Egon Schiele, who in May 1915 was called up in spite of health problems to take up duties as a clerk in a camp for Russian prisoners at Mühling near Wieselburg in Lower Austria. His unusual drawing of the office at the camp (one of a pair) foregrounds his box of chalks, pen and pencils on an empty table (cat. 7). The inclusion of the stove, the closed door with its unreadable calendars and maps and the empty spaces in this sparse linear drawing serve to project an air of quiet warmth, comfort and somnolence. Not much action is called for here except for visual dreaming.

Drawing the drawer: deceptive views of solitude and witness

Even when we look at nature, our imagination constructs the picture —Eugène Delacroix[49]

Drawn records of wild and seemingly undisturbed nature are often marked by a small solitary figure depicted from the rear, the *Rückenfigur*.[50] These little, observing artists

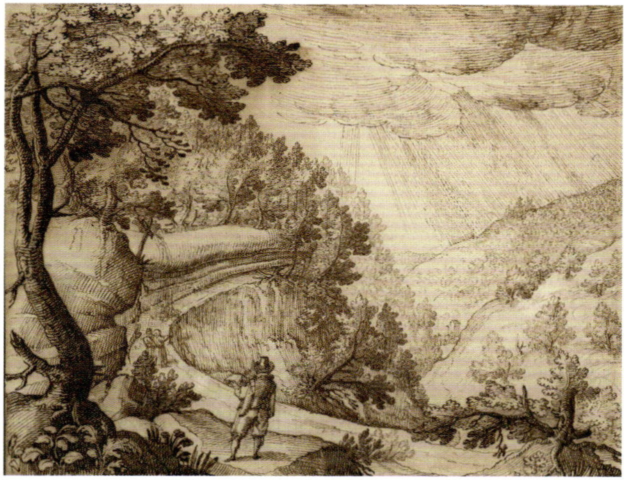

FIG. 11
Remigio Cantagallina (c. 1582–1656), *Artist sketching a landslide*, pen and brown ink over black chalk, 192 × 252 mm, Katrin Bellinger collection, inv. no. 2015-028

are usually bent over a sketchbook or board with total absorption. More than the standard 'staffage' figures included in landscape to provide scale, these drawers serve as a potent reminder to the viewer that 'nature' is a construct. Acting as a mediator between spectators of the artwork and the view being recorded within the picture, the solitary *Rückenfigur* contradictorily signifies the companionable aspect of most travel and sketching trips throughout the centuries. However much these memes of witness to a significant cultural journey appear to be alone, another artist has been present to record their presence!

In a drawing by draughtsman and etcher Remigio Cantagallina of a standing figure surveying a landslide (fig. 11), the drawer turns his back to the viewer to record the ravished landscape. Heavy storm clouds releasing streams of rain are interspersed with rays of sunshine over the distant slopes, and two monks are also out on the curved road to witness the damage. Cantagallina, like his master Giulio Parigi (1571–1635), travelled to the Low Countries and was heavily influenced by Paul Bril (c.1553–1626), the Antwerp-born artist who spent many years in Rome. Cantagallina draws in pen and ink, framing views with heavy swirling foliage on one side of the work in the manner of a theatrical set, with distanced vistas open to the other side of the framed page in lighter pen work. The emphatic use of thick pen lines in the Bril manner produces extremely stylised foliage and generic forms, which present nature as a narrative fiction rather than a scene of geographical accuracy. Nevertheless, in his Netherlands travel sketchbook of 1612–13 (Musées Royaux des Beaux-Arts de Belgique, Brussels, inv. no. 2994), Cantagallina recorded extremely precise wash drawings of buildings, landmarks and city sites.

The tiny drawing figure in the foreground of a *Landscape with an artist sketching* (cat. 1), now attributed to the Master of the Mountain Landscapes, participates in a delicate evocation of coded alpine peaks and valleys. Together with a companion looking over his shoulder, he is almost lost in a flurry of pen markings, dispatched evenly over the page so that no aspect of rocks, trees, mountains, valleys, water and sky is given priority – and certainly not the diminutive travellers. This work was formerly attributed to Roelant Savery (1576–1639), and prior to that was believed to be by Pieter Bruegel the Elder (c.1525/30–1569), possibly commemorating an alpine journey made on his return to the Low Countries from his stay in Italy during the 1550s.

There is a close connection between Roelant Savery, previously named as an author of the above-mentioned alpine landscape, and Rembrandt's one-time pupil Lambert Doomer. In 1658, Doomer acquired the volume of Savery's drawings of his journey through the Tyrol which had been in Rembrandt's collection, and made copies of some of these works.[51] As an observant traveller, Doomer celebrated his companionable peregrinations around France in 1646 with the artist Willem Schellinks (1627–1678) in a number

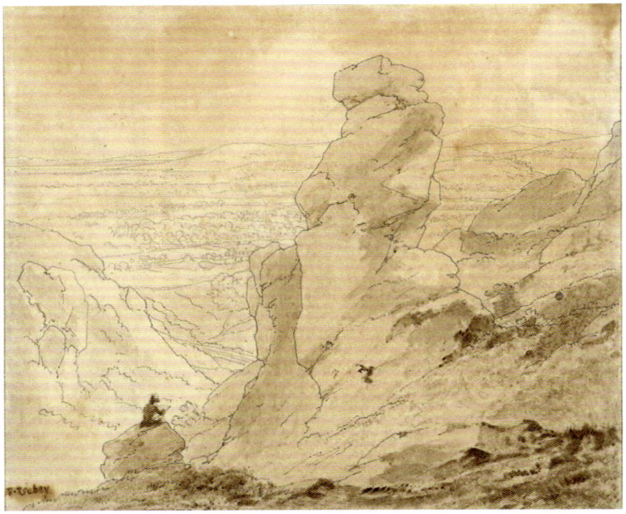

FIG. 12
Jean-Baptiste Isabey (1767–1855), *Valley of Saint Helena near Baden, with an artist sketching*, 1812, graphite, pen and grey ink, brown wash, 147 × 199 mm, Katrin Bellinger collection, inv. no. 2001-001

of pen-and-wash drawings showing an artist sketching in the landscape or ruins.[52] The beautiful little drawing of an anonymous drawing artist (cat. 2) is very much in the Rembrandt tradition, maximising the contrast between free linear markings in bold reed pen and suave washes of warm brown ink. The artist with his tall hat sits on a bank under a tree, his figure taut with concentration. The open space between the foreground artist and the wintry bank of trees he is drawing informs us of the scale and complexity of nature that artists need to compress into a tiny sketchbook format. The amateur artist and jurist Jan de Bisschop, who was a fierce critic of Rembrandt, employs an almost identical pose in a wonderfully assured small wash drawing (cat. 3). Seated on the ground, each on a small cushion, but drenched with warm sun, two artists are carefully drawing a bust of Lysimachus, the Greek successor to Alexander the Great.[53]

Associated with all these drawings are tales of shared journeys, artistic pilgrimages and celebratory excursions. Sketching trips became particularly popular in the eighteenth century for professionals and amateurs, as witnessed in the unfinished watercolour of *The Colosseum from the Palatine Hill* by Carlo Labruzzi (cat. 4). Johann Wolfgang Goethe was to write enthusiastically from Frascati in 1786 in his Roman diaries:

> *For two days we have roamed the countryside, always finding some new attraction. Yet I find it hard to decide which are the more entertaining, our days or our evenings* [...] [*when*] *we sit down in a circle and each brings out the drawings and sketches he has made during the day.*[54]

During his travels in Italy in 1761 with the abbé de Saint-Non, mentioned above, Fragonard met up with Hubert Robert, associated with the French Academy in Rome. Their red chalk drawings of landscapes, ruins and antiquities made during companionable travels were closely aligned and Robert utilised his sketchbook material during the rest of his career. He peopled his semi-fantastical landscapes and classical sites with figures observed and imaginary, and very often included a drawing artist, as did Fragonard. In a time when artists were usually trained in academies, the incidental sketching person in these works evokes that diagrammatic figure traced in printed perspective manuals from whose eyes radiate the geometrical lines of spatial construction. A view, a *veduta*, demands an eye as well as the skill to construct it convincingly!

Robert delighted in the contradictory readings of grand classical ruins and contemporary bucolic interventions in France and Italy: makeshift dwellings, carts, animals, shepherds and children disport themselves amongst fallen statuary and coffered vaults. So in the drawing *An artist drawing beside a statue of Jupiter* (cat. 6), the tricorne-hatted artist, who has seated himself in a wooden wheelbarrow in order to achieve a happily foreshortened view of the

Capitoline Jupiter, is probably only as 'real' as the half-imagined setting.[55] The very tall ladder might have been recently used by him to get a better view of the noble statue, probably covered with dust, droppings and the detritus of desuetude, like the companion sculptural figures in a curved decorated niche that has become a storage space for wine barrels and rotting straw. Nevertheless, the mood of this drawing is light-hearted and, although they are abandoned, the wine barrels evoke Bacchic pleasures.

The exaggeration of scale conditioned by the picturesque, the sublime or the romantic context is given deliciously preposterous emphasis in a small drawing (fig. 12) by Jean-Baptiste Isabey. The French landscape and genre painter Isabey was strongly influenced by Eugène Delacroix (1798–1863), although he studied with Jacques-Louis David (1748–1825). Vastness and roughness are 'powerful causes' of the sublime, according to Edmund Burke,[56] and discussions of sublimity continued to be of interest to Delacroix, who questioned the conflation of sublimity ('that which is highest, which reaches to the skies') and perfection in a late *Journal* entry: 'The best way of discovering the sublime is to polish one's work less'.[57] There are certainly no remnants of David's polish and finish in Isabey's view of the Saint Helena Valley in the Wienerwald range in Austria near Baden bei Wien. He has transformed this relatively tame landscape into a wild and turbulent place of romantic drama, with the little artist in the foreground impossibly perched on an exaggerated outcrop drawing in sublime insecurity.

An introspective activity

The charming Neoclassical drawing by Fanny Guillaume de Bassoncourt of an unknown woman artist at her easel (cat. 16) is the work of an extremely skilful amateur. The manner in which she has depicted the subject's coiffure from behind, piled on top of a bent neck into a carefully shaded tall ring of plaits and side ringlets, implies an intimate and affectionate knowledge of the sitter's body. The artist's overdress with its discretely shaded drapery, protective sleeves and high belt is described with a controlled linearity, allowing for certain emphases of limited shadow in the paint dabs on the square easel and the patterning on an underskirt and cushion on her chair. Her preliminary sketch, which she would have made *en plein air*, is fixed to the top of the easel so that she can easily refer to it while working on the canvas below, and her box of paints is to hand on the right.

In the eighteenth and nineteenth centuries drawing as a polite and useful art was an essential accomplishment for the middle and aristocratic classes in most European societies with access to private tutors, and was necessary for all those engaging in the cultural pilgrimage to Rome. Participants of the Grand Tour often took classes from Italian drawing masters as well as participating in excursions to classical sites or renowned beauty spots.[58] In France, despite beliefs that a woman's place was only in the domestic sphere, wealthy or aristocratic women exercised considerable cultural influence through their literary salons and their published commentaries and essays on the annual artistic Salon after its establishment as a public event.[59] Women's participation as exhibiting artists in the Salon grew as high as 192 by 1835, and represented about 22 per cent of the total by the end of the nineteenth century.[60] Women mainly worked in minor genres such as still life, flower, landscape and genre painting, being excluded from the study of the nude considered essential for history pictures (female students were only admitted into the Ecole nationale des Beaux-Arts in 1897). But, as has been noted, these were 'the very genres that were gaining the favour of art-buying public who left the acquisition of history and religious painting to official Institutions'.[61] The drawing by a very young Fanny Guillaume de Bassoncourt – whether amateur or professional – celebrates the seriousness and absorption of the artist at work, as well as satisfying historical notions of discreet feminine charm for the spectator. The figure at the easel retains her elegance in this cultivated, but nonetheless absorbing, pursuit.

The same can be said of a very precocious watercolour inscribed on the verso *Tom Heywood/ age 21 years/ Art student/August 1868* (fig. 13). It depicts elegant back-views of two women drawing at a table in a well-equipped drawing school. The long view from a vestibule through an open door and wide expanse of floor to the women absorbed in their task acts as a witty compositional device to separate and exclude us from their activity. Unlike the Pericles bust, which appears to turn with some animation on its angled plinth, the artists are too engrossed to look up or notice our presence. Pericles was associated with the Classical Age of Athens so his inclusion serves to signify the *civilitas* of their activities. The drawing school is hung with architectural friezes, prints and drawings, flower pieces for copying and casts of the *Medici Venus* and a full-size *Spinario*. The picture attests to the seriousness of art activities, whatever the gender or professional status of pupils or practitioners.

Representing working artists from the rear constitutes the reverse of the mirror doubling in the (inevitably) frontal self-portrait of an artist, such as the compelling *Self-portrait with pencil and sketchbook* (1924) by Lovis Corinth (cat. 17). The intermittent activity of looking up to the mirror and down to the drawing block or sketchbook has resulted in changes of angle in the sloping of the head, the eyes, ears and mouth, in the way the face projects over shifting shoulders and in the redrawing of the hands and fluid proportions of the lower part of the body. These shifts and breaks have added to the vitality and intensity of the drawing, assisted by the free pencil lines and insistent overdrawing. Corinth suffered a stroke in 1911 and his prolific self-portraits in pencil, paint, etching and lithography grapple with facial distortion with a ruthless lack of self-pity. The intensity of his gaze grinds through the pencil markings to the exclusion of the spectator.

Drawing other participants in the act of drawing is just as much a reflexive activity as the self-focused portrait in a mirror. Artists at work is not a simple subject about a mechanical activity: it is a reflection on creativity, history, self-identity and, inevitably, drawing's protean ability to encompass finish and unfinish and link beginnings and endings by virtue of its linearity.

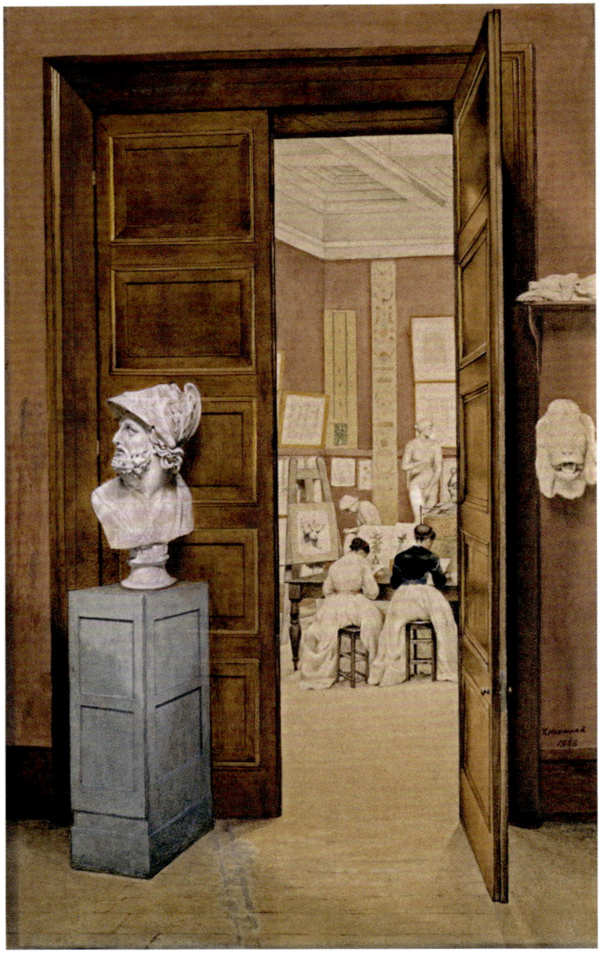

FIG. 13
Tom Heywood (active 1868–1913), *Two ladies in a drawing school*, 1868, watercolour, 441 × 278 mm, Katrin Bellinger collection, inv. no. 1990-003

1 P. Gosset, *Henri Harpignies*, Ghent, 1982, cited (without page reference) by Vincent Pomarède in *Tradition & Revolution in French Art 1700–1880: Paintings & Drawings from Lille* (exh. cat., London: National Gallery Publications, 1993), p. 142.

2 The various *topoi* associated with artists' self-representations are examined in some detail in Deanna Petherbridge, *The Primacy of Drawing; Histories and Theories of Practice* (New Haven and London: Yale University Press, 2010), pp. 287–345.

3 Vasari's friend and adviser Vincenzo Borghini, for example, makes a distinction between *fatica* and *invenzione* in his unpublished 'Selva di notizie'. See Stuart Currie, '*Invenzione, disegno e fatica*: two drawings by Giovambattista Naldini for an altarpiece in post-Tridentine Florence', in *Drawing 1400–1600: Invention and Innovation*, ed. Stuart Currie (Aldershot and Vermont: Ashgate, 1998), pp. 151–53. Of the many discussions about the distinction between the 'mechanical' and the 'intellectual' in the formation of the Académie Royal de Peinture et de Sculpture in seventeenth-century France, see Thomas Puttfarken, *The Discovery of Pictorial Composition: Theories of Visual Order in Painting 1400–1899* (New Haven and London: Yale University Press, 2000), pp. 229–43.

4 *Sir Joshua Reynolds: Discourses on Art*, ed. Robert R. Wark (New Haven and London: Yale University Press, 1975), p. 45.

5 See G.C. Mariani et al., *Luca Evangelista: Parola e immagine tra Oriente e Occidente* (exh. cat., Padua: Diocesan Museum, 2000); and Gisela Kraut, *Lukas mält die Madonna: Zeugnisse zum künstlerischen Selbstverständnis in der Malerei* (Worms: Wernersche Verlagsgesellschaft, 1986).

6 The raised head of Saint Luke, even in the act of writing, as he appears in some images of the Four Evangelists, evokes this aspect of inspired listening; see, for example, Jacopo Pontormo's tondo of *Saint Luke* in the pendentive of the Capponi Chapel, Church of Santa Felicita, Florence, dated 1525–28.

7 An Italo–Byzantine icon of this type sits on a shelf in Giovanni Lanfranco's painting of *Saint Luke* (1611), formerly in the Collegio Notarile in Piacenza, although it does not appear in the preparatory drawing discussed below in the text.

8 See Michele Bacci, *Il pennello dell'Evangelista: Storia delle immagini sacre attribuite a San Luca* (Pisa: GISEM Edizioni ETS, 1998).

9 The original version is in the Museum of Fine Arts, Boston, and there are close copies in the Groeningemuseum, Bruges (c.1491–1510); the Hermitage Museum, Saint Petersburg (c.1440); and the Alte Pinakothek, Munich (c.1484). See *Rogier van der Weyden, Luke Drawing the Virgin: Selected Essays in Context* (Boston: Museum of Fine Arts and and Turnhout: Brepols, 1997).

10 For information on the Antwerp Guild of Saint Luke, see Zirka Zaremba Filipczak, *Picturing Art in Antwerp 1550–1700* (Princeton, NJ: Princeton University Press, 1987), pp. 11–19.

11 See Jan Piet Filedt Kok, *De Heilige Lucas tekent en schildert de Madonna* (Amsterdam: Vossiuspers, 2006). For example, an altar panel by Hugo van der Goes (c.1470–80) in the Museu Nacional de Arte Antiga, Lisbon, depicts a genuflecting Evangelist drawing with a metalpoint tool on a piece of paper resting on a book, while a piece of charcoal, a sharpening tool and a quill pen are visible on the floor next to him.

12 Two notable Mannerist examples are by Jan Gossaert, called Mabuse (c.1472–1532). The Evangelist and Virgin share the same Italianate architectural interior in the painting *Saint Luke drawing the Virgin* (c.1513–15), previously on the main altar of Sanct Veit (Saint Vitus) Cathedral, Prague, and now in the Národní Galerie Prague. In the later version *Saint Luke painting the Virgin* (c.1520–25), in the Kunsthistorisches Museum, Gemäldegalerie, Vienna (inv. no. 894), the Virgin floats before the genuflecting Evangelist in a mandorla lit by a warm, if spectral, light and surrounded by floating and winged putti. He draws with a stylus on a sheet resting on a board.

13 Jan de Beer, *Saint Luke painting the Virgin and Child* (c.1504–09), Pinacoteca di Brera, Milan, inv. no. 672.

14 *Jan de Beer. Gothic Renewal in Renaissance Antwerp* (Turnhout: Brepols, 2016), pp. 89–94, 338. De Beer is listed in Lodovico Guicciardini's *Descrittione* (1567) of Netherlandish panel painters, an important source for Vasari's *Lives*. According to Dan Ewing, however, de Beer does not appear in the reduced list in the expanded edition of Vasari's *Lives*; see Dan Ewing, 'Jan de Beer's Lifetime Reputation and Posthumous Fate', *Journal of Historians of Netherlandish Art*, 7: 2 (Summer 2015), DOI: 10.5092/jhna.2015.7.2.1 [accessed 21 November 2017].

15 Vasari painted a fresco cycle of scenes derived from Pliny in his houses in Arezzo and Florence; the monochrome series in Arezzo survives in better condition.

16 Nicholas Turner relates this drawing to a painting from 1611, formerly in the Collegio Notarile of Piacenza (mentioned above) and now in the Musei Civici of the city; see Nicholas Turner, *Italian Drawings in the British Museum: Roman Baroque Drawings c.1620 to c.1700*, vol. 1 (London: British Museum Press, 1999), pp. 107–108. Although the drawing is designated *Saint Luke painting the Virgin*, the Evangelist does not hold a brush, but rather a drawing tool, in his hand.

17 The image of Saint Luke surrounded by angels is in one of the scenes of the Four Evangelists in the pendentives of the central dome of the Church of Holy Apostles, Naples, painted by Lanfranco in the 1640s.

18 C.L. Joost-Gaugier, 'The Early Beginnings of the Notion of "Uomini Famosi" and the "De Viris Illustribus" in Greco-Roman Literary Tradition', *Artibus et Historiae*, 3: 6 (1982), pp. 97–115. Fra Luca Pacioli (c.1447–1517) published a number of mathematical works before his *De divina proportione* (written in the late 1490s and published in Florence in 1509) which include illustrations of complex solids provided by Leonardo da Vinci (1452–1519).

19 P.A. Emison, *Creating the 'Divine' Artist from Dante to Michelangelo* (Leiden and Boston: Brill, 2004), p. 4.

20 See the useful and comprehensive historiography of *ingegno* in Emison, *Creating the 'Divine' Artist*, pp. 73–87.

21 Chapters V, VI and VII in Federico Zuccaro, *L'idea de'pittori, scultori ed architetti* (Turin, 1607); excerpts can be found in *Scritti d'arte di Federico Zuccaro*, ed. Detlef Heikamp (Florence: L.S. Olschki, 1961). The 1768 publication of this text has been digitised and can be accessed at: https://archive.org/stream/lideadepittoriscoozucc#page

22 See Rona Goffen, *Renaissance Rivals: Michelangelo, Leonardo, Raphael, Titian* (New Haven and London: Yale University Press, 2004).

23 Pliny, *Natural History Books XXXIII–XXXV* (Loeb Classical Library), trans. H. Rackham (Cambridge, MA, and London: Harvard University Press, 1999), p. 327. For a discussion of Lucian's text, see David Cast, *The Calumny of Apelles: A Study in the Humanist Tradition* (New Haven and London: Yale University Press, 1981). Botticelli's *Calumny of Apelles* (c.1494) is in the Gallerie degli Uffizi, Florence, and Zuccaro's oil painting *Calumny* (c.1569–72) is in the Royal Collection, Windsor Castle. For further details of the latter, see Lucy Whitaker and Martin Clayton, *The Art of Italy in the Royal Collection: Renaissance & Baroque* (London: Royal Collection Publications, 2007) pp. 76–79.

24 The work denounced the critical detractors of Zuccaro's ill-fated commission for the church of the Madonna del Baraccano in Bologna, the Pope's home town. Zuccaro's assistant Domenico Cresti, called Passignano (c.1560–1636), was also tried on 12 November, 1581. Passignano had addressed the subject of *Saint Luke painting the Madonna* in the Gallerie degli Uffizi, with the Virgin as an apparition floating in the sky above an enormous vertical canvas before which the Evangelist performs the act of painting.

25 The Christ Church drawing of *Porta Virtutis* is believed to be the earliest of three existing versions. The other two are in the Morgan Library & Museum, New York and the Städel Institute, Frankfurt. It has been suggested that the later versions could have been drawn during his trial. See James Byam Shaw, *Drawing by Old Masters at Christ Church, Oxford*, 2 vols. (Oxford: Oxford Clarendon Press, 1976), I, p. 155; II, no. 544; and E.J. Mundy and E. Ourusoff de Fernandez-Gimenez, *Renaissance into Baroque. Italian Master Drawings by the Zuccari, 1550–1600* (exh. cat., Milwaukee Art Museum, Milwaukee and New York 1989), pp. 252–55.

26 Figures of evil intent as well as benign personifications of Prudence, Temperance, Virtue and so on would become stock iconographic personifications in Baroque compilations, such as Andrea Alciati's 1531 *Emblemata*, the *Iconologia* of Cesare Ripa from 1593, and Vincenzo Cartari's 1615 *Imagini degli Dei de gl'Antichi*, which references Federico's *Calumny of Apelles.*

27 Slanted hailstones appear in Albrecht Dürer's iconic etching, *Witch riding backwards on a goat* (1500), as well as in many later representations of envy and witchcraft; see Deanna Petherbridge, *Witches & Wicked Bodies* (Edinburgh: National Galleries of Scotland, 2013), and 'Leaky Vessels and Devil's Dugs', in *Visions of Enchantment: Occultism, Spirituality and Visual Culture*, ed. Daniel Zamani and Judith Nobel (London and New York: Fulgur, 2018).

28 The cross of Saint James was conferred on him in 1530 by the Holy Roman Emperor Charles V; see Adriano Aymonino and Anne Varick Lauder, *Drawn from the Antique: Artists & the Classical Idea* (exh. cat., Sir John Soane's Museum, London, 2015), pp. 89–93.

29 The inscription reads MICHAEL-A[N]GELUS-BONAROTUS-FLORENT[INUS]-FACIEBA[T]. See a discussion of the 'Plinian signature as a Badge of Prestige' in Sarah Black McHam, *Pliny and the Artistic Culture of the Italian Renaissance: The Legacy of the Natural History* (New Haven and London: Yale University Press, 2013), pp. 183–203.

30 McHam, *Pliny and the Artistic Culture of the Italian Renaissance*, p. 183.

31 Pliny, *Natural History, XXXVI*: 86, pp. 324–25. In Vasari's fresco *Apelles and the Cobbler,* Casa Vasari, Florence (c.1569–73), Apelles is depicted eavesdropping on the comments of four visitors while hiding behind a large canvas on an easel.

32 Pliny, *Natural History XXXVI*: 86, pp. 324–25.

33 Angela Cipriani, 'L'Accademia di San Luca dai concorsi dei giovani ai concorsi Clementini', in Anton W.A. Boschloo et al., *Academies of Art between Renaissance and Romanticism* ('S-Gravenhage: SDU Uitgeverij, 1989), pp. 61–76.

34 I am grateful to Anita Viola Sganzerla for sharing this research with me prior to publication.

35 On the album in the Louvre, see Isabelle Compin, 'Une nouvelle identification iconographique d'un dessin d'Oudry', *Lettre des Amis du Musée des Beaux-Arts de Lille*, 43 (1994), pp. 2–3.

36 *Le Voyage d'Italie de Charles-Nicolas Cochin* (1758), ed. Christian Michel (Rome: Ecole Française de Rome, 1991), p. 351; cited in Perrin Stein et al., *Drawing Triumphant: Works from New York Collections* (exh. cat., The Metropolitan Museum of Art, New York, 2016), p. 116.

37 Jean-Honoré Fragonard, *Study after Giovanni Lanfranco: Saint Luke surrounded by angels (from the Church of the Holy Apostles, Naples)* (1760–61), The Norton Simon Foundation, Pasadena, California (inv. no. F.1970.03.02a-b.D). Fragonard also made a print after this same painting by Lanfranco (c.1761–65), an impression of which is in the British Museum (inv. no. 1882,0311.1152).

38 M.D. Sheriff, *Fragonard: Art and Eroticism* (Chicago and London: University of Chicago Press, 1990), pp. 146–47.

39 See Yuriko Jackall et al., *Fragonard: The Fantasy Figures* (exh. cat., National Gallery of Art, Washington, D.C., 2017).

40 Sheriff, *Fragonard*, p. 162.

41 An old label on the back of the painting in the Louvre (inv. no. M.I. 1061) states 'Portrait of Mr l'abbé de Saint Non, / painted by Fragonard, / in 1769, in one hour's time' [sic].

42 Stein, *Drawing Triumphant*, pp. 54–55.

43 'In depictions of saints, enthusiasm was conceived as Christian fervor, but in secularized representations of artists or writers, enthusiasm was cast in terms of self-contemplation [....] Maintaining the traditional pose attests to the power of visual conventions both to endure and to change'; see Sheriff, *Fragonard*, p. 157.

44 Dusart had also drawn and printed a series of *The Five Senses*, where sight (*Gesigt*) is illustrated by a woman in a tall headdress holding a candle to her face so that three grotesque peasant admirers can leer at her, including a bearded ancient holding identical spectacles above his drooling open mouth.

45 See *Adriaen van Ostade, die schönsten Radierungen; und eine Auswahl aus dem Werk seiner Nachfolger Cornelis Bega, Cornelis Dusart u.a.* (exh. cat., C.G. Boerner, New York, 1985).

46 www.slub-dresden.de/sammlungen/deutsche-fotothek/fotografen/donadini/ [accessed 1 December, 2017]. Tiepolo-style ceilings appear framed in a photograph of Donadini's studio (see fig. 18).

47 The Emperor William II, who staged a state funeral for Menzel, referred to him as 'the posthumous Apelles of Old Fritz', meaning Frederick the Great; cited in Françoise Forster-Hahn, 'Adolph Menzel: readings between nationalism and modernity', in *Adolph Menzel 1815–1905: Between Romanticism and Impressionism*, ed. Claude Keisch and Marie Ursula Riemann-Reyher (New Haven, London and Washington D. C.: Yale University Press, in association with the National Gallery of Art, Washington, D.C., 1996), p. 103.

48 Recorded in the review *Die Gegenwart* (1897) and cited in Peter-Klaus Schuster, 'Menzel's modernity', in Keisch and Riemann-Reyher, *Adolph Menzel*, p. 140.

49 *The Journal of Eugène Delacroix*, trans. Lucy Norton (London: Phaidon Press, 1995), p. 415.

50 Joseph Leo Koerner, *Caspar David Friedrich and the Subject of Landscape* (London: Reaktion, 1990), pp. 162–66. See also Petherbridge, *The Primacy of Drawing*, pp. 302–08.

51 Wolfgang Schulz, 'Doomer and Savery', *Master Drawings*, 9 (Autumn 1971), p. 25.

52 Petherbridge, *The Primacy of Drawing*, pp. 307–08.

53 Aymonino and Varick Lauder, *Drawn from the Antique*, pp. 140–42.

54 Johann Wolfgang von Goethe, *Italian Journey (1786–1788)*, trans. W.H. Auden and Elizabeth Mayer (Harmondsworth: Penguin Books, 1970), p. 138. Ludwig Tieck's influential tale of artistic travels, *Franz Sternbald's Wanderungen, eine altdeutsche Geschichte*, was published in Berlin ten years later, in 1798, with contributions from Wilhelm Heinrich Wackenroder.

55 The semi-domed circular structure evokes centralised spaces such as the domed chapel or the underground rotonda in the Palazzo Farnese at Caprarola, near Viterbo, which Robert visited in 1761 and 1764; see Jean de Cayeux, *Les Hubert Robert de la Collection Veyrene au Musée de Valence* (Valence: Le Musée de Valence, 2000), pp. 99–103.

56 'Greatness of dimension, is a powerful cause of the sublime [....] A perpendicular has more force in forming the sublime than an inclined plane; and the effects of a rugged and broken surface seem stronger than where it is smooth and polished': see Edmund Burke, *A Philosophical Enquiry into the Sublime and Beautiful*, ed. David Womersley (London: Penguin Books, 1998), p. 114.

57 *The Journal of Eugène Delacroix*, p. 392.

58 The key texts outlining these practices are Kim Sloan, *'A Noble Art': Amateur Artists and Drawing Masters c.1600–1800* (exh. cat., British Museum, London, 2000), and Ann Bermingham, *Learning to Draw: Studies in the Cultural History of a Polite and Useful Art* (New Haven and London: Yale University Press, 2000).

59 For the development of the salon exhibition in the eighteenth century, see Thomas E. Crow, *Painters and Public Life in Eighteenth-Century Paris* (New Haven and London: Yale University Press, 1985): and for women's participation, *Women Art Critics in Nineteenth Century France: Vanishing Acts*, ed. Wendelin Guentner (Newark: University of Delaware Press, 2013). The growing literature in this area includes *Femininity and Masculinity in Eighteenth-century Art and Culture*, ed. Gill Perry and Michael Rossington (Manchester: Manchester University Press, 1994).

60 Véronique Chagnon-Burke, 'A Career True to Woman's Nature: Constructing the Woman Artist in France's Midcentury Feminine Press', in Wendelin Guentner, *Women Art Critics*, p. 119.

61 Chagnon-Burke, 'A Career True to Woman's Nature', p. 120.

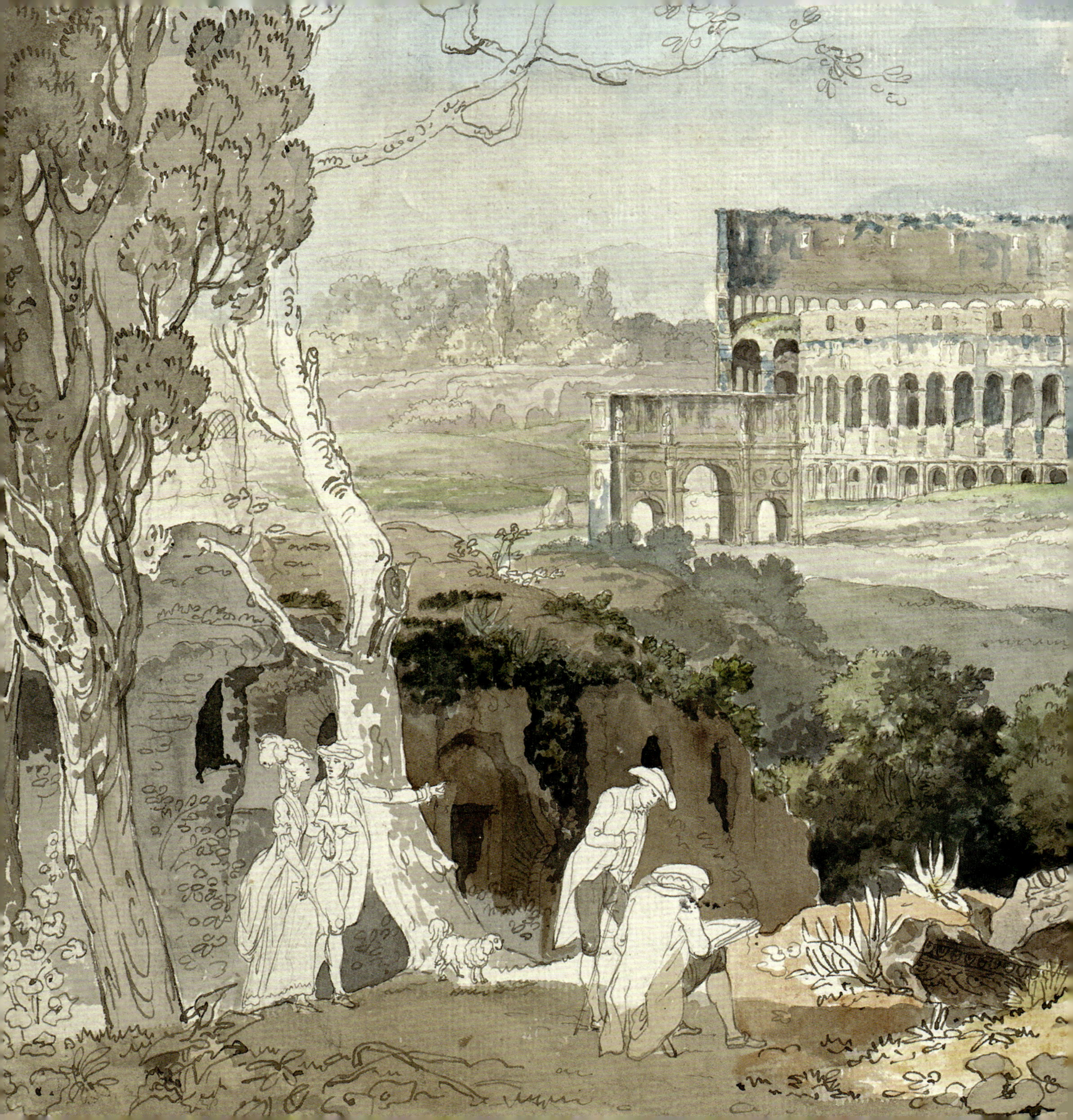

Catalogue

BY ANITA VIOLA SGANZERLA

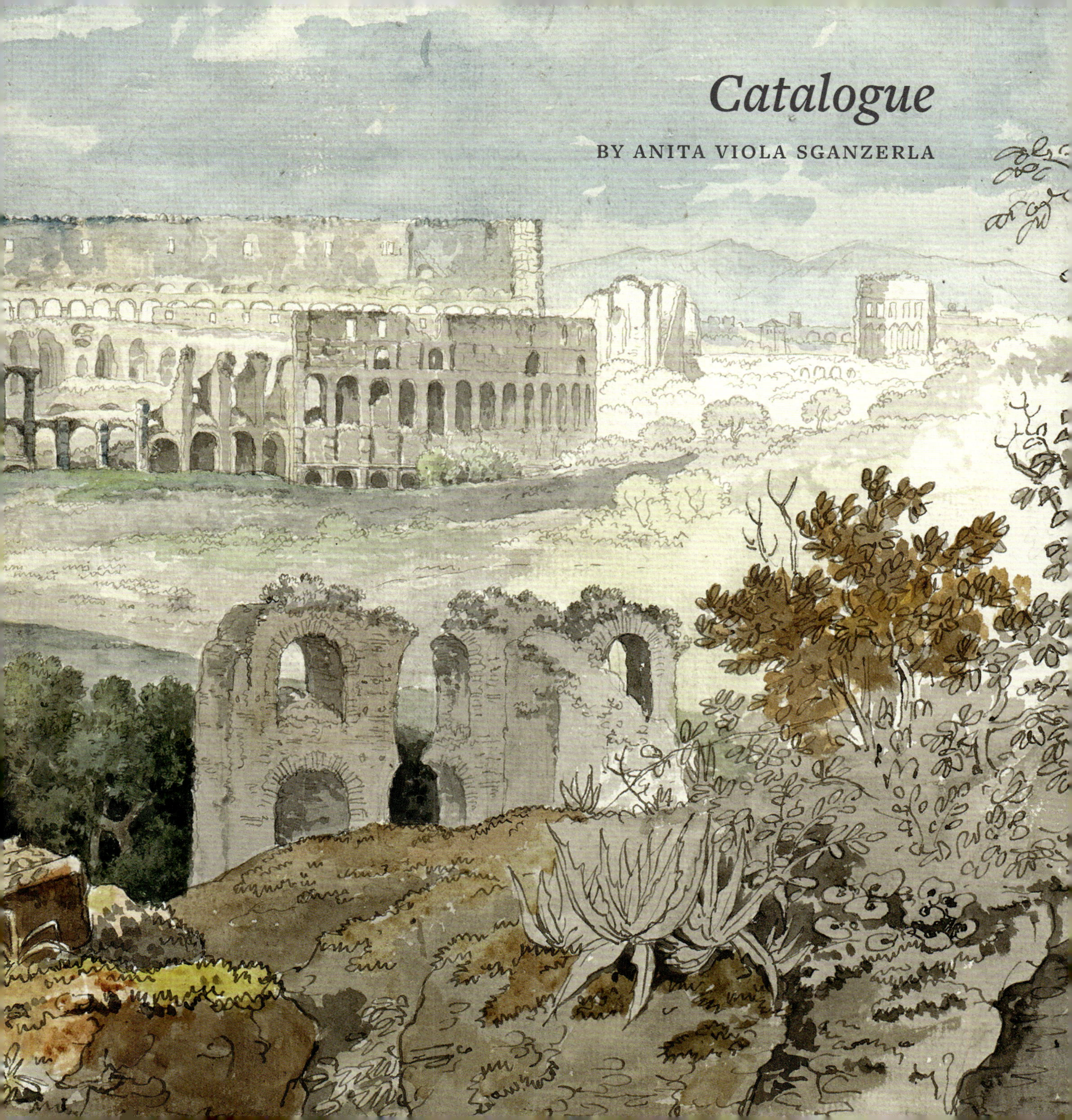

1

MASTER OF THE MOUNTAIN LANDSCAPES (active late 16th or early 17th century)

Landscape with an artist sketching c. 1606–08

Black chalk, pen and brown ink, 277 × 396 mm
The Courtauld Gallery, London, inv. no. D.1978.PG.9

Within the vast expanse of a mountain valley, an artist at work sits by a large rock while a companion looks over his shoulder. Deftly rendered, in spite of their minute size, the two figures, seen from behind, complete and complement the detailed depiction of this magnificent landscape. Through their inclusion in the scene, the two figures allude to the practice of drawing outdoors – thus possibly hinting at the execution of the sheet itself. In addition, their act of observing the scenery parallels the beholder's own act of looking, in a conceptual overlap between physical and drawn landscape. Meticulously carried out in pen and ink, this drawing combines passages of minute stipple-like strokes with confidently hatched areas of shading. The interplay of the two serves to convey the illusion of a long-distant view. Aside from the two tiny figures, no other sign of human presence is included, allowing the draughtsman to focus exclusively on the rendition of the hills, trees, lake and mountain-tops.

Its subject-matter, and the subtle play between natural and picturesque landscape, bring this intriguing drawing close to the realm of Pieter Bruegel the Elder (1525/30–1569), to whom the sheet was originally ascribed.[1] Bruegel made several pen-and-ink drawings of Alpine landscapes following his journeys to and from Italy between 1551 and 1554. Although close in tone to Bruegel's accepted sheets, the present work, together with several others, was first reattributed to Roelant Savery (1576–1639), and most recently to the Master of the Mountain Landscapes, an anonymous artist whose drawing style is close to Bruegel's and Savery's. This change in attribution is supported by formal differences and by the appearance, on some of the sheets in the group, of the Strasbourg Lily watermark, found on paper dating from the mid-1580s through the seventeenth century, thus too late for them to have been executed by Bruegel.[2]

INSCRIPTIONS Inscribed, lower left, *de ouden Bruegel,* and on the verso, *den ouden Bruegel no.56*

PROVENANCE Possibly Joris Hoefnagel (1542–1601); part of an album compiled in England, around 1800; W. Thompson; from whom acquired by Colnaghi (London), 26 September 1948; from whom acquired by Count Antoine Seilern, London (1901–1978), on 28 October 1948; accepted in lieu of tax by HM Government and presented to the Home House Society (now the Samuel Courtauld Trust) in 1981; The Courtauld Gallery

EXHIBITIONS *The Princes Gate Collection – Drawings (Selection A)*, The Courtauld Gallery, London, 1982, no. 126; *Mantegna to Cézanne – Master Drawings from the Courtauld*, The British Museum, London, 1983, no. 20; *Master Drawings from the Courtauld Collections*, The Courtauld Gallery, London, 1991, no. 14

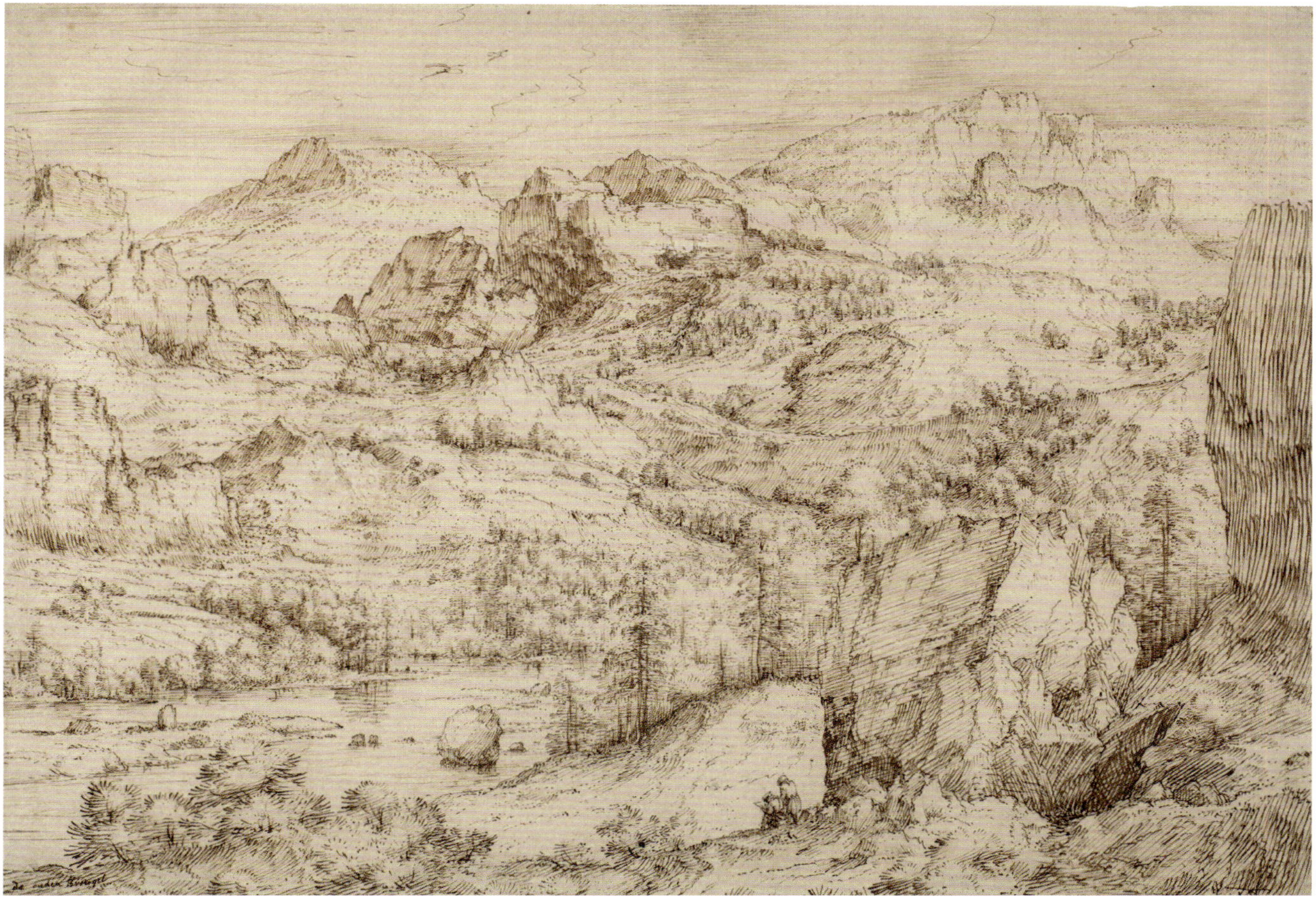

2

LAMBERT DOOMER (Amsterdam 1624–1700 Amsterdam)

An artist seated by a tree, sketching early 1660s

Pen and brown ink, brown wash, 145 × 117 mm
Katrin Bellinger collection, inv. no. 1992-001

Born in Amsterdam in 1624, Lambert Doomer initially trained as a wood carver under his father, the cabinetmaker Harmen Doomer (1595–1650). He soon moved to drawing and was probably placed under the guidance of Rembrandt – one of his father's customers – in whose studio he may have worked around 1645–46.[1] He subsequently travelled through France in 1646 and in Germany around 1663, where he executed numerous topographical drawings made from nature, specialising in landscapes which feature architectural elements. In 1657–58, at Rembrandt's bankruptcy sale, Doomer acquired a large number of works by the master together with part of his art collection, including an album containing drawings by Roelant Savery.

Deftly executed in pen and ink with extensive application of wash, this accomplished small drawing of an artist sketching outdoors seated by a tree is a mature work by Doomer.[2] A distinctive feature of his draughtsmanship, brown wash is layered on most of the sheet, producing subtle atmospheric effects.

In pose and outfit, the draughtsman in this drawing resembles one such figure in Doomer's *The fountain at Cleves, with an artist sketching*, in the British Museum (fig. 14).[3] Datable to c. 1663, the year Doomer travelled in the Rhine region, the British Museum sheet documents his visit to the newly built Tiergarten on the Springenberg at Cleves. Laid out under the local Stadholder, Prince Johan Maurits of Nassau-Siegen (1604–1679), today little remains of this picturesque complex. Also datable to the mid-1660s, the present figure study was probably made to be reused for a larger composition. Indeed, the same draughtsman, seen from behind, reappears in Doomer's *View of Bacharach with Stahleck Castle*.[4]

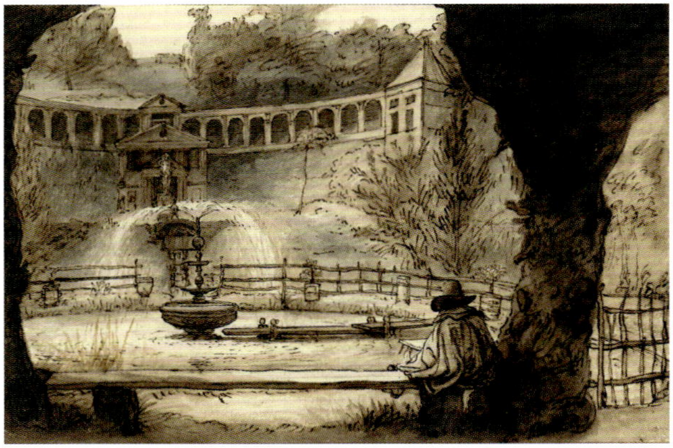

FIG. 14
Lambert Doomer, *The fountain at Cleves, with an artist sketching*, c. 1663, pen and brown ink with grey and brown wash over graphite, touched with yellow-brown wash, The British Museum, London, inv. no. 1886,1012.539

PROVENANCE Robert von Hirsch, Basel; his sale, Sotheby's, London, 20 June 1978, lot 36; anonymous sale, Sotheby's, New York, 14 January 1992, lot 92, at which acquired

EXHIBITION *Handzeichnungen alter Meister aus Deutschem Privatbesitz*, Frankfurt, Städelsche Kunstinstitut, 1924, p. ix, ill. pl. V (as Gerbrand van der Eeckhout)

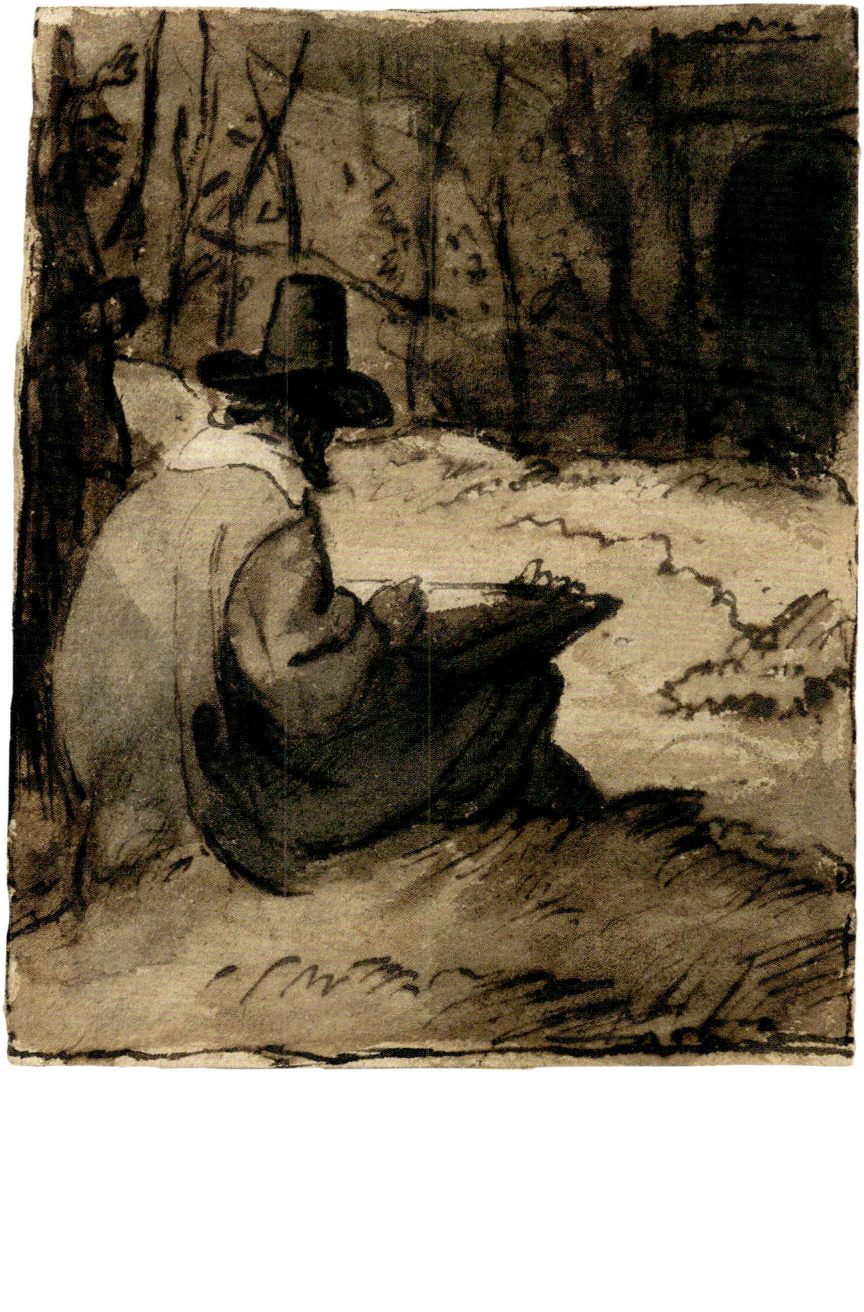

3

JAN DE BISSCHOP (Amsterdam 1628–1671 The Hague)

Two artists drawing an antique bust (recto)
A reclining man seen from the back (verso, not illustrated) c. 1660

Pen and brown ink, brown wash, 91 × 135 mm
Watermark: Arms of Amsterdam (fragment)
Katrin Bellinger collection, inv. no. 1992-012

Representations of artists working outdoors are not exclusive to landscape drawing, as exemplified by this charming sketch by Jan de Bisschop.[1] Here, in a sun-drenched exterior, two draughtsmen seen from behind are intent on studying an antique bust, nowadays identified as an effigy of Lysimachus, the Greek successor to Alexander the Great. Then thought to represent a philosopher, plaster casts of this much-copied bust were in circulation in the seventeenth century.

Most likely drawn from life, the present sheet may once have been part of a portable sketchbook, just like the one being used by the draughtsman on the right. The drawing excursions that de Bisschop took in the company of his friend and fellow artist Constantijn Huygens the Younger (1628–1697) were the likely inspiration for two closely comparable drawings, one by each artist, both featuring a pair of draughtsmen seated outdoors.[2] While both artists' pen drawings are notable for their swiftness of execution and the skilful application of ink wash, in the present sheet de Bisschop has excelled in imbuing the scene with a palpable glow.

A contemporary of Lambert Doomer (see cat. 2), de Bisschop was a lawyer by profession and an artist by passion. His talents ranged from drawing and etching to writing and connoisseurship. A passionate scholar of antiquity, he contributed to the introduction of drawing both from antique sculpture and from the model as a component of artistic training in The Hague. Amongst his published works, the *Signorum veterum icones* (1668–69) was specifically aimed at inspiring art students to learn from the best examples of classical statuary.[3]

INSCRIPTIONS Inscribed, lower right, in pencil, *J. Bisschop*

PROVENANCE Private collection, Germany; sale, Sotheby's, London, 13 April 1992, lot 260, at which acquired

EXHIBITIONS *Drawings related to Sculpture, 1520–1620*, Katrin Bellinger at Harari & Johns, London, 1992, n. p.; *Drawn from the Antique. Artists & the Classical Ideal*, Sir John Soane's Museum, London, 2015, no. 13

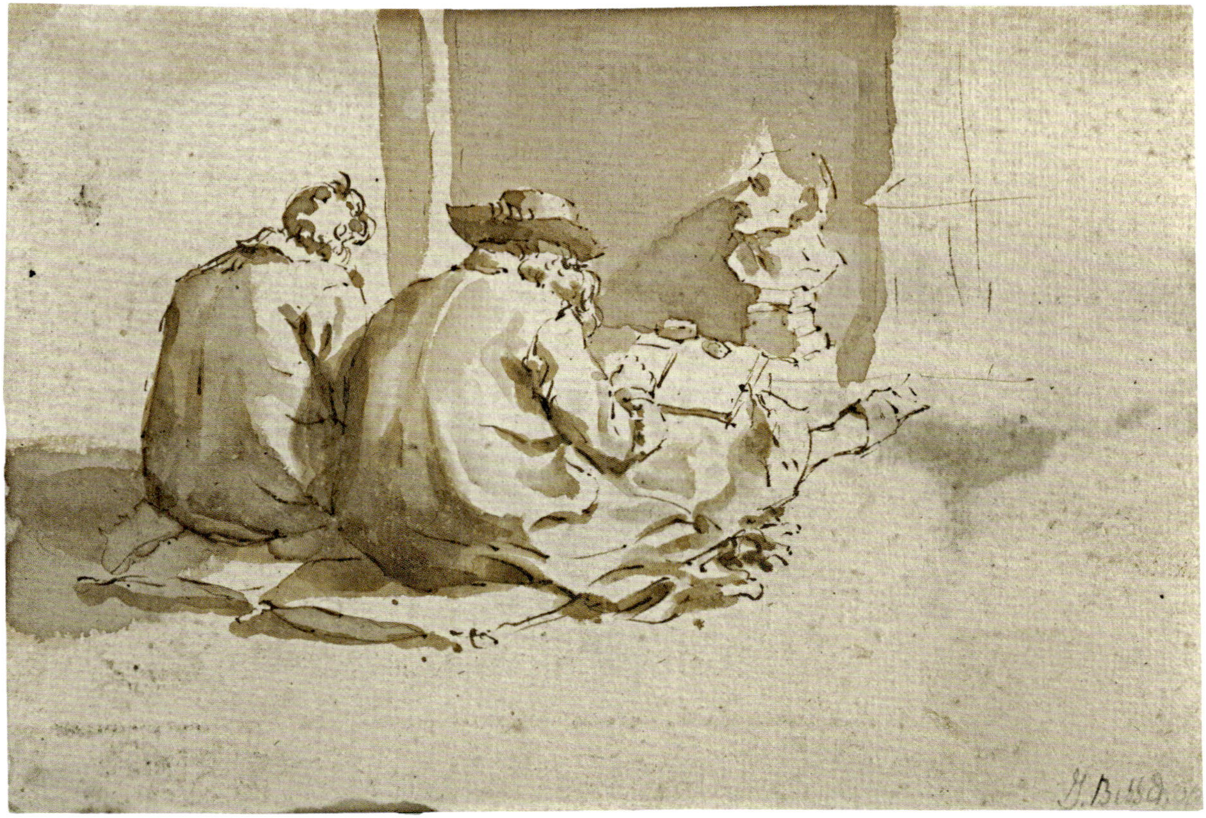

4

CARLO LABRUZZI (Rome 1748–1817 Perugia)

The Colosseum seen from the Palatine Hill, Rome, a pair of tourists with their cicerone, and an artist sketching

Graphite, pen and brown and grey ink, watercolour, 375 × 540 mm
Watermark: J HONIG / ZOON
Katrin Bellinger collection, inv. no. 2012-017

The Roman painter, draughtsman and engraver Carlo Labruzzi is best known for his panoramic views of Rome and its surroundings. This beautifully preserved drawing, possibly made in the late 1760s or early 1770s, shows a view of the Imperial Forum taken from the gardens of the English College, on the Palatine Hill. The Colosseum, seen from the south, is flanked on the left by the Arch of Constantine. In the distance to the right, we see the Baths of Trajan against the backdrop of the Sabine Hills.[1] An elegantly attired lady approaches from the left. She is accompanied by a *cicerone*, a knowledgeable local guide charged with enriching her visit to Rome with all manner of historical and anecdotal flourishes. To the right of the pair, the sketching artist and his companion are probably meant to represent Labruzzi and one of his aristocratic patrons. This scene is one commonly associated with the experience of the young noblemen and women of the Grand Tour, who visited Rome as one of the highlights of their extended travels across Italy, France, Germany and the Low Countries.

Working first *en plein air* and later in the studio, Labruzzi would delineate his compositions in pencil, later strengthening the lines in pen and ink and adding layers of watercolour in a variety of hues. The varying degrees of finish between background and foreground, or landscape and figures, add to the allure and the luminous quality of the sheet. Labruzzi's panoramic views of the most popular tourist spots catered for the contemporary antiquarian taste and fascination with the classics and gained particular favour amongst British collectors. Probably carried out as an independent work, the present drawing shows the same view and figures as one of Labruzzi's paintings, although in the latter the scene is set at twilight.[2]

INSCRIPTIONS Inscribed, on the mount, *Colliseum* [sic] *from the Palatine Hill*

PROVENANCE From one of two albums compiled by the artist and acquired from his widow in 1818 by the 1st Lord Wharncliffe (1776–1845); then by descent to the 3rd Lord Wharncliffe (1892–1953); his wife Lady Elfreda Mary Fitzwilliam (1898–1979); then by descent to the 8th Earl Fitzwilliam (1910–1948); his sale, Wentworth Woodhouse, Rotherham, Yorkshire, 1948; private collection; Simon C. Dickinson, Ltd, London, 2012, from whom acquired

EXHIBITION *Carlo Labruzzi. The Grand Tour*, Dickinson, London, 2012, no. 5

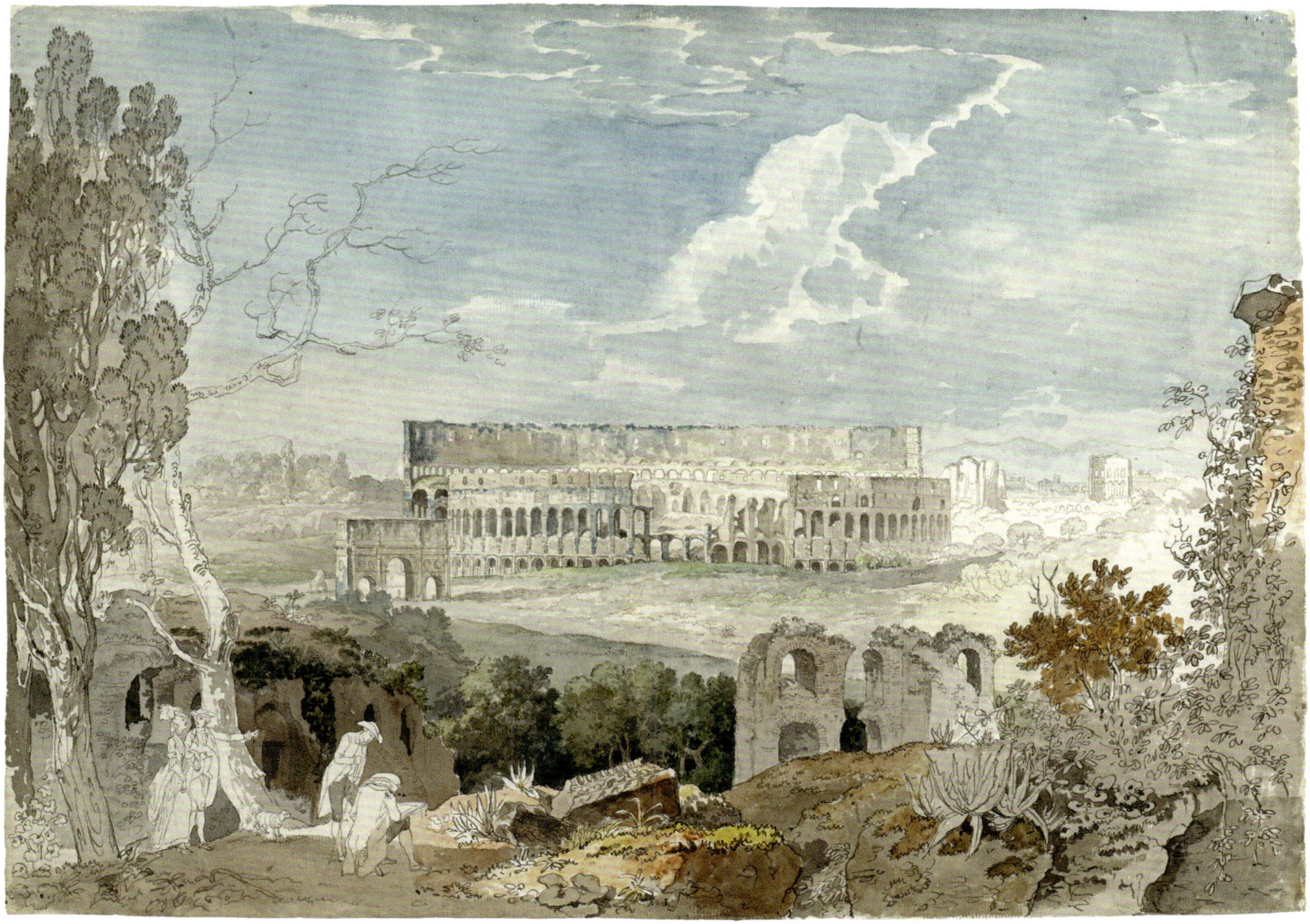

5

GEORG EDUARD GEHBE (Meiningen 1845–1920 Salzburg)

A painter in a forest, surprised by a deer

Graphite, 300 × 220 mm
Katrin Bellinger collection, inv. no. 1995-056

The painter and draughtsman Georg Eduard Gehbe was born in 1845 in Meiningen, Thuringia, in central Germany.[1] He initially studied with Friedrich Preller the Elder (1804–1878) in Weimar. Following periods in Berlin, Paris and Switzerland, he lived in Vienna, where he was a pupil of Albert Zimmermann (1808–1888) and Hans Canon (1829–1885). After a stay in Hungary he returned to Vienna but settled in Salzburg in 1884. Two years later he set up his studio there, in the newly built Künstlerhaus (Artists' house). Gehbe established himself as a highly respected member of the Salzburg school, specialising in mountain and forest landscapes, hunting still lifes, genre scenes and portraits.

Characteristic of Gehbe's forest scenes, this drawing demonstrates his debt to Preller, both compositionally and stylistically.[2] Preller's landscape drawings are characterised by a somewhat dry and controlled modelling of natural forms.[3] Similarly, Gehbe's composition is dominated by the pair of large tree-trunks that span from bottom left to top right, structurally anchoring the scene. This sylvan glade is not disrupted by the centrally placed small figure of an artist – perhaps a romanticised self-portrait – who sits on the ground by his easel, at the edge of a small creek. Startled and delighted by the sudden appearance of a deer elegantly jumping past him, the painter spreads his arms, while still holding his mahl-stick and palette. This picturesque encounter is balanced by Gehbe's restrained drawing style. Aside from a few darker passages where he has applied more pressure to his pencil, the sheet is overall even in tone. He has exploited the silvery quality of graphite, set against the areas of untouched white paper, to convey the gentle play of light and shade on the forest's intricate patterns of thick foliage and branches.

INSCRIPTIONS Signed on a rock, lower left, *Gehbe*

PROVENANCE Thomas Le Claire Kunsthandel, Hamburg, 1995, from whom acquired

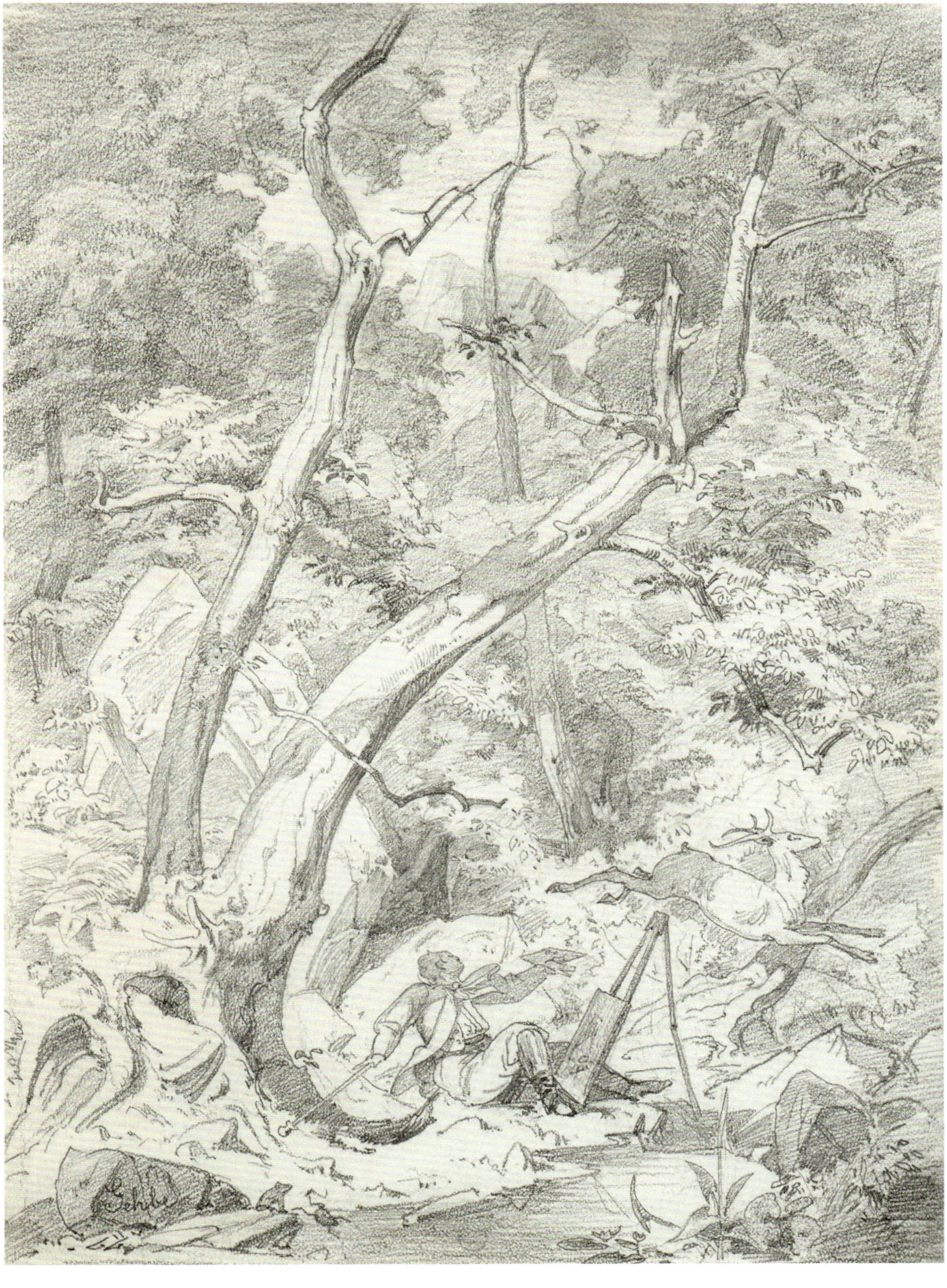

6

HUBERT ROBERT (Paris 1733–1808 Paris)

An artist drawing beside a statue of Jupiter 1762

Red chalk, 530 × 400 mm
Katrin Bellinger collection, inv. no. 1989-006

Typical of Hubert Robert's Roman drawings, this large sheet shows the small figure of a draughtsman in a tricorne hat, atop a wheelbarrow, sketching a monumental statue of the Capitoline Jupiter.[1] A pile of discarded wine barrels, overgrown with vegetation, takes up the right-hand side of the composition. An old shovel and rake have been leant against Jupiter's pedestal together with a tall ladder. The architectural backdrop, a rotunda with niches populated with antique statues, recalls those represented in other sheets by Robert, such as *A rotunda inspired by the Baths of Diocletian*, dated 1761, in Valence.[2] The statues may also include, aside from Jupiter, an Aesculapius and a fragment of a statue of Diana accompanied by a dog.

A precise identification of the site and antiquities was not, however, Robert's primary concern. As attested by the sheet's swiftness of execution, it was conceived as a display of Robert's skills as a draughtsman and a free variation on motifs capable of evoking the pleasure of discovering Rome's forgotten grandeur. Our drawing belongs to a small group of red chalk drawings, datable to 1762, of which counterproofs exist that have been reworked by one of Robert's contemporaries in Rome, Jean-Robert Ango (active between c. 1760 and c. 1773).[3]

A second sheet in the Katrin Bellinger collection (fig. 15) is a reworked counterproof of the present drawing, or, more

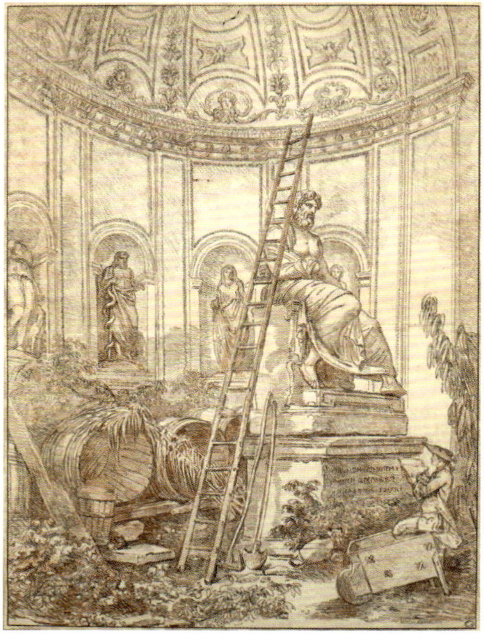

FIG. 15
Jean-Robert Ango and Hubert Robert, *An artist drawing beside a statue of Jupiter*, c. 1763–64, black chalk counterproof over red chalk counterproof, reworked in black chalk, 500 × 380 mm, Katrin Bellinger collection, inv. no. 1990-005

INSCRIPTIONS Signed, located and dated, on the pedestal of Jupiter's statue [...] / *H. Roberti a*[?] *Roma /1762* [...]

PROVENANCE Anonymous sale, Hôtel Drouot, Paris, 10 June 1911, lot 149; sale, Sotheby's, Monaco, 2 December 1989, lot 203, at which acquired

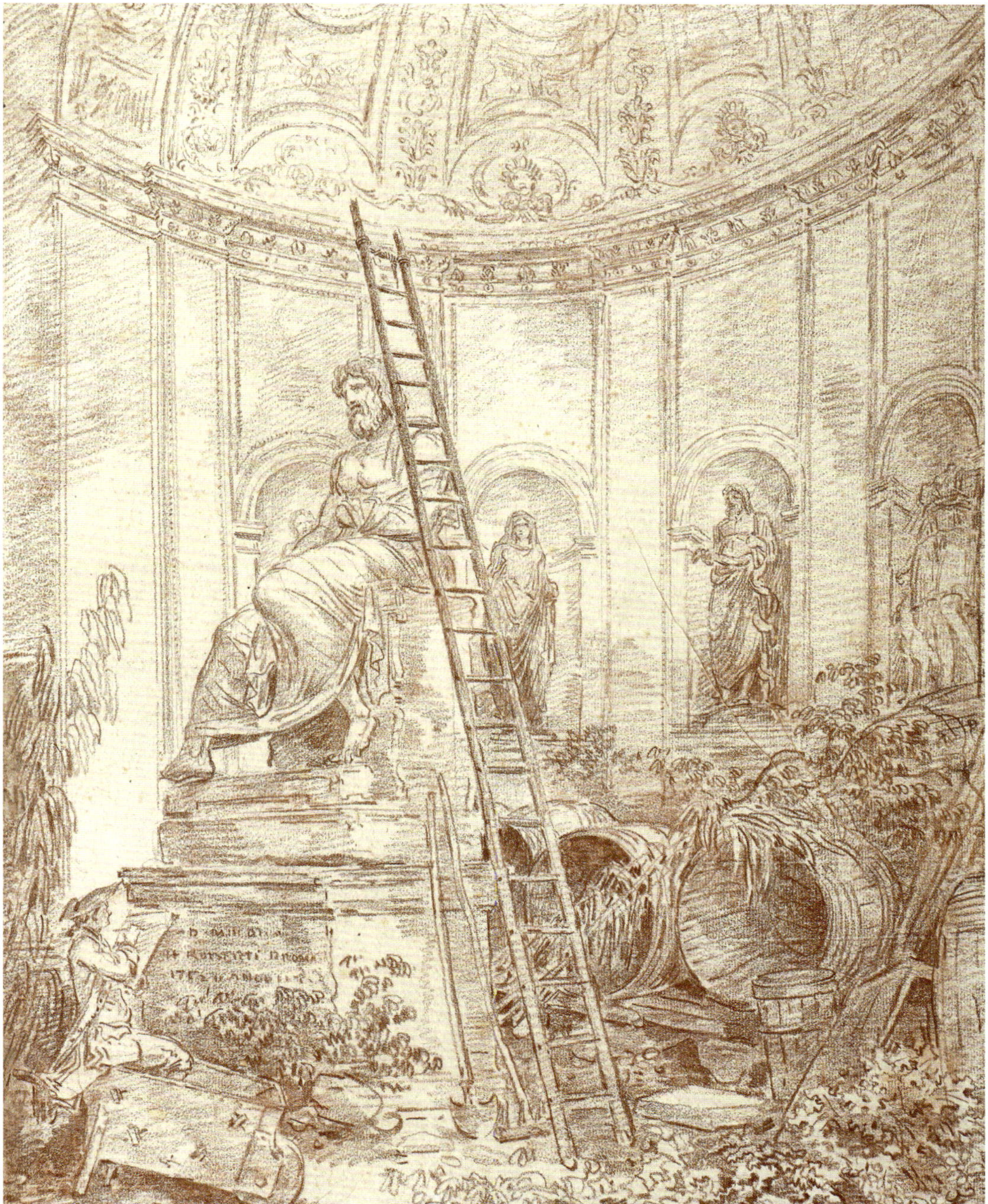

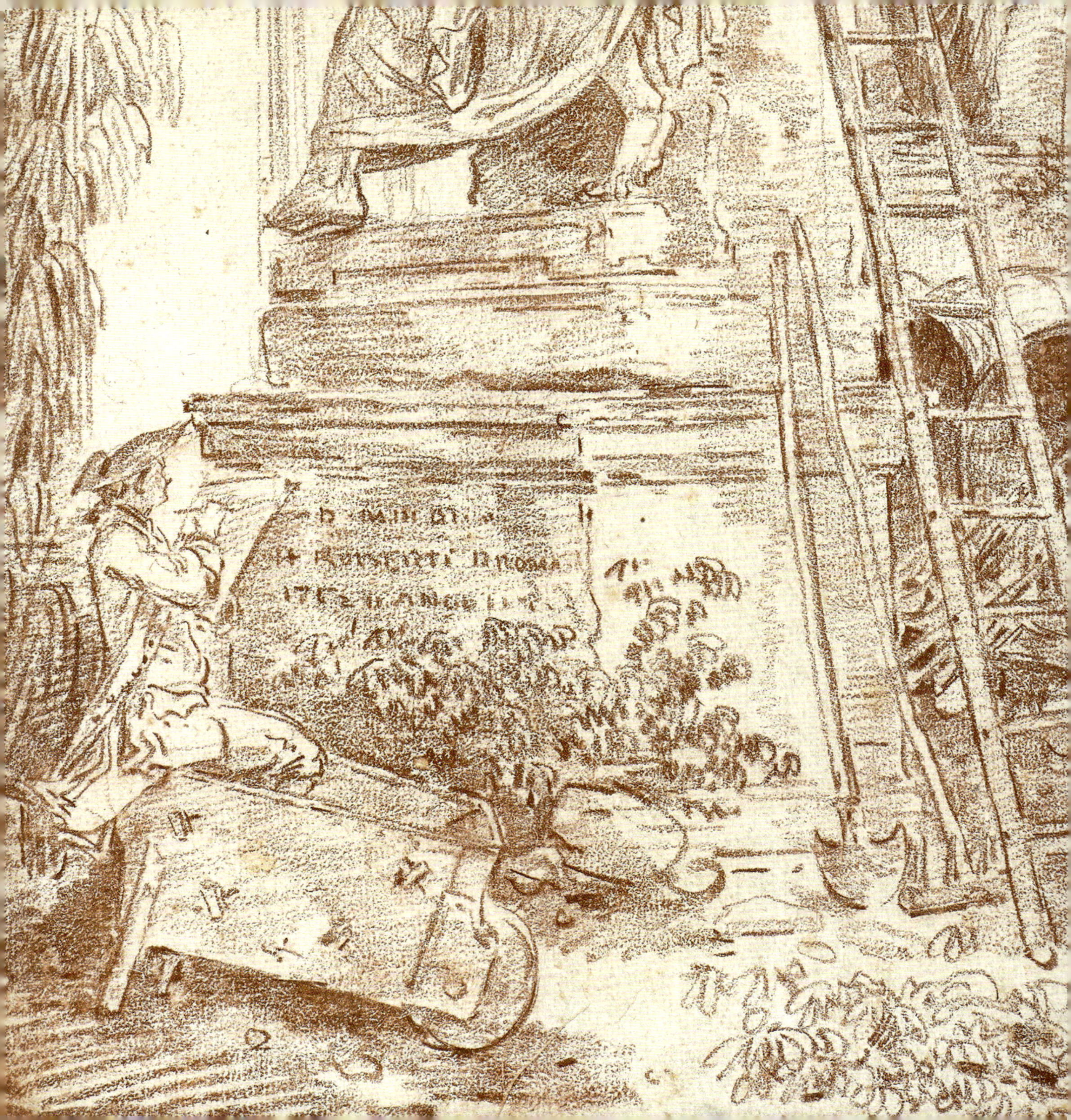

precisely, a 'counterproof on a counterproof'.[4] The process may be summarised as follows: Robert executed a drawing in red chalk and immediately pulled a counterproof – or offset – of it, while the chalk was still fresh. Ango would then have made a copy in black chalk of Robert's original, of which a counterproof would be pulled, not on a fresh sheet of paper, but superimposing it on the red chalk counterproof. At this point, Robert's counterproof was ready for Ango to add some finishing touches in black chalk, such as strengthening some of the details and making adjustments (to counter the effects of image reversal), as in the case of our drawing, where a few deft strokes serve to ensure that the draughtsman is sketching with his right hand. Arguably resulting from some sort of working relationship between Robert and Ango, such reworked counterproofs combined fashionable subject-matter with technical inventiveness and may have been intended either to be sold or to fulfil a commission.[5]

7

EGON SCHIELE (Tulln 1890–1918 Vienna)

Office at the Mühling prisoner-of-war camp 1916

Black and red crayon, 461 × 292 mm
Katrin Bellinger collection, inv. no. 2013-031

Egon Schiele was drafted into the Austrian Army in June 1915, shortly after having married Edith Harms. Owing to his weak constitution, he never served at the front. After his training, in March 1916, he was sent to Atzgersdorf, near Liesing, where Russian prisoners were housed in an abandoned factory. While on guard duty, Schiele made compassionately drawn portraits of his charges, to whom he felt united by a common longing for peace.[1] In May 1916, a new placement was found for the artist, the office job he had been hoping for. Schiele had been begging to be sent to Vienna but was instead transferred to a prisoner-of-war camp in Mühling, a small village near Wieselburg, three hours west of the city, which felt to him very remote. As clerk of the supply office, Schiele was in charge of keeping the account books for the camp, a role he was assigned because of his very elegant handwriting.

In spite of his initial disappointment, this placement afforded Schiele relative comfort. Since Mühling was not in a war zone, Edith was allowed to join him, and they lived together in a cottage close to the army base. Moreover, his superiors supported his creative needs as best as they could. The first lieutenant, Gustav Hermann, even assigned him an empty storeroom to use as a makeshift studio. Although the space was small, it served both as office and as an art studio, as illustrated in this beautiful drawing and in its companion piece, now in the Leopold Museum, Vienna.[2] While in the Vienna drawing Schiele focused on his desk and the orderly arrangement of objects on it, in the present drawing he stepped away from it to capture his cramped quarters in their entirety, including the piled table and a stove in the corner. A toolbox filled with pens and pencils, the tools of both the clerk and the draughtsman, occupies the foreground and contributes to the drawing's intimate scale. Stripped of extraneous detail, with measured touches of red crayon to emphasise a few sparse objects, this is a rare occurrence of a still life in Schiele's oeuvre.

INSCRIPTIONS Signed and dated, lower centre, *EGON / SCHIELE / 1916* (inscribed into a rectangle)

PROVENANCE Egon Seefehler, Vienna; Galerie Würthle, Vienna; estate of Serge Sabarsky, New York, by 1968;[3] private collection, from which acquired in 2013

SELECTED EXHIBITIONS *Gustav Klimt and Egon Schiele*, The Solomon R. Guggenheim Museum, New York, 1965, no. 57 (addenda); *Gustav Klimt – Egon Schiele: Zum Gedächtnis ihres Todes vor 50 Jahren*, Graphische Sammlung Albertina, Vienna, 1968, no. 258; *Egon Schiele: vom Schüler zum Meister*, Akademie der bildenden Künste, Vienna, 1984, no. 88; *Egon Schiele: 100 Zeichnungen und Aquarelle*, Städtische Galerie Rosenheim, Rosenheim, 1988, no. 80; *Egon Schiele: cent œuvres sur papier*, Musée Granet, Aix-en-Provence, 1993, no. 79; *Egon Schiele. The Ronald S. Lauder and Serge Sabarsky Collections*, Neue Galerie, New York, 2006, no. D138; *From Klimt To Klee: Masterworks from the Serge Sabarsky Collection*, Neue Galerie, New York, 2010, no. 48

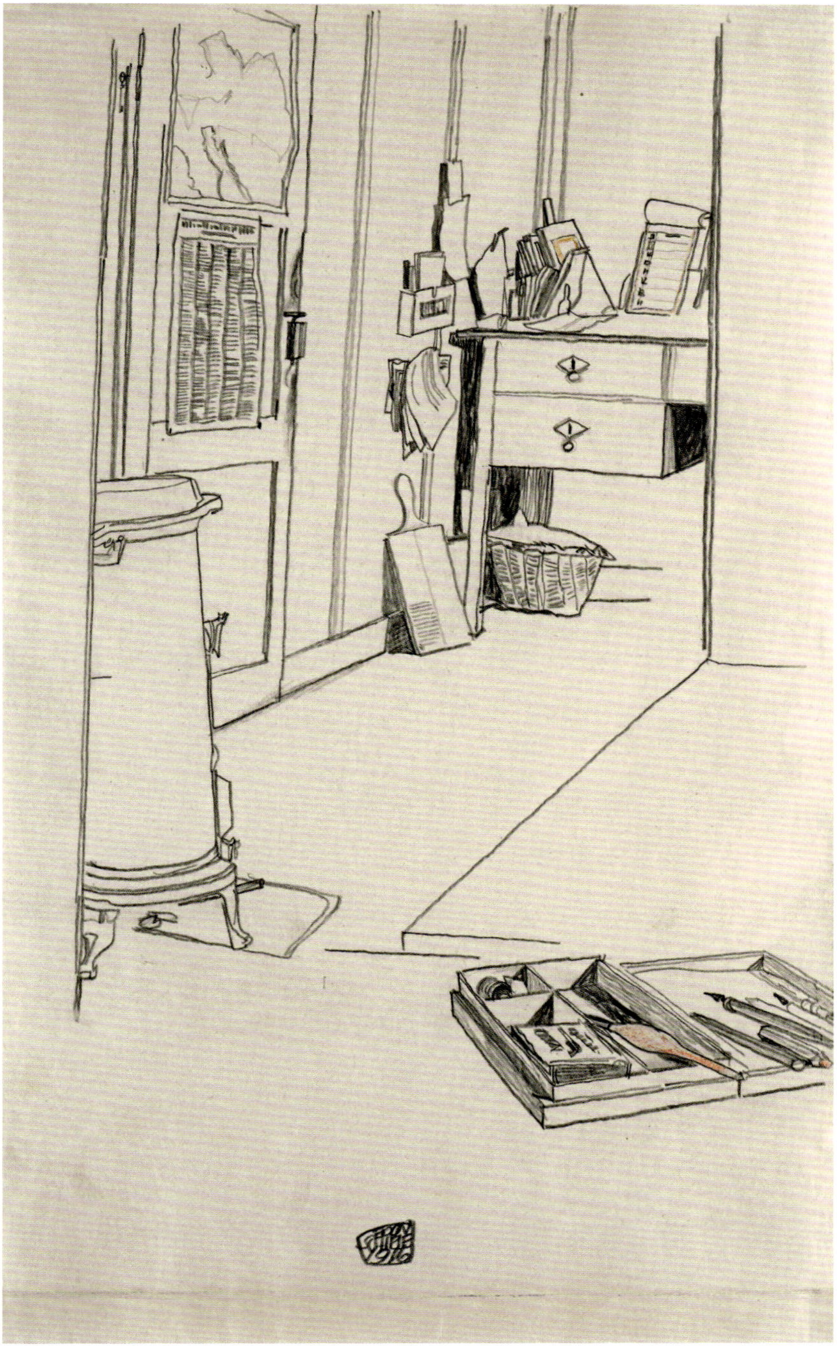

8

ANONYMOUS (FRENCH SCHOOL?)

An artist's studio with a covered easel 1896

Black chalk (and charcoal?) with stumping, 600 × 440 mm
Katrin Bellinger collection, inv. no. 1997-022

This large, highly worked drawing shows a partial view of an interior. Although the scene is visually dominated by a large double-sided easel with its base pushed right up against a wall, it is not immediately clear whether we are looking at an artist's studio. The canvas on the easel is turned to face inwards. As if this did not suffice to hide it from view, the canvas and the top of the easel are shrouded in draped fabric.

A large wardrobe, topped by a sculpted bust, stands in the corner of the room with a room-divider right next to it. This may be a screen of the kind used by models to prepare themselves for a sitting. Partially obscured by the easel, several paintings and drawings, both framed and unframed, hang on the wall. Supported by wooden rails, the three drawings at the lower centre present some curious features. They are each divided in half by a vertical line. Their format recalls the page-spread of an album. Could they be copies after a drawing manual, perhaps one devoted to the study of perspective?[1]

Both the wardrobe and the elegant side table, which holds a lamp and books, bring to mind a domestic interior. This may then be a living space that doubles as an artist's studio, perhaps that of an amateur artist. Clearly defined areas of unmarked paper convey the brighter passages, and the draughtsman has carefully delineated the texture of the drapery. Although proficiently executed, this anonymous drawing may be the work of a non-professional or aspiring artist, perhaps done as an exercise in the rigorous rendering of volumes and placement of shadows.

INSCRIPTIONS Indistinctly signed and dated, lower left, in graphite, *Mel / Nov 96*

PROVENANCE Hazlitt, Gooden & Fox, London, 1997, from whom acquired

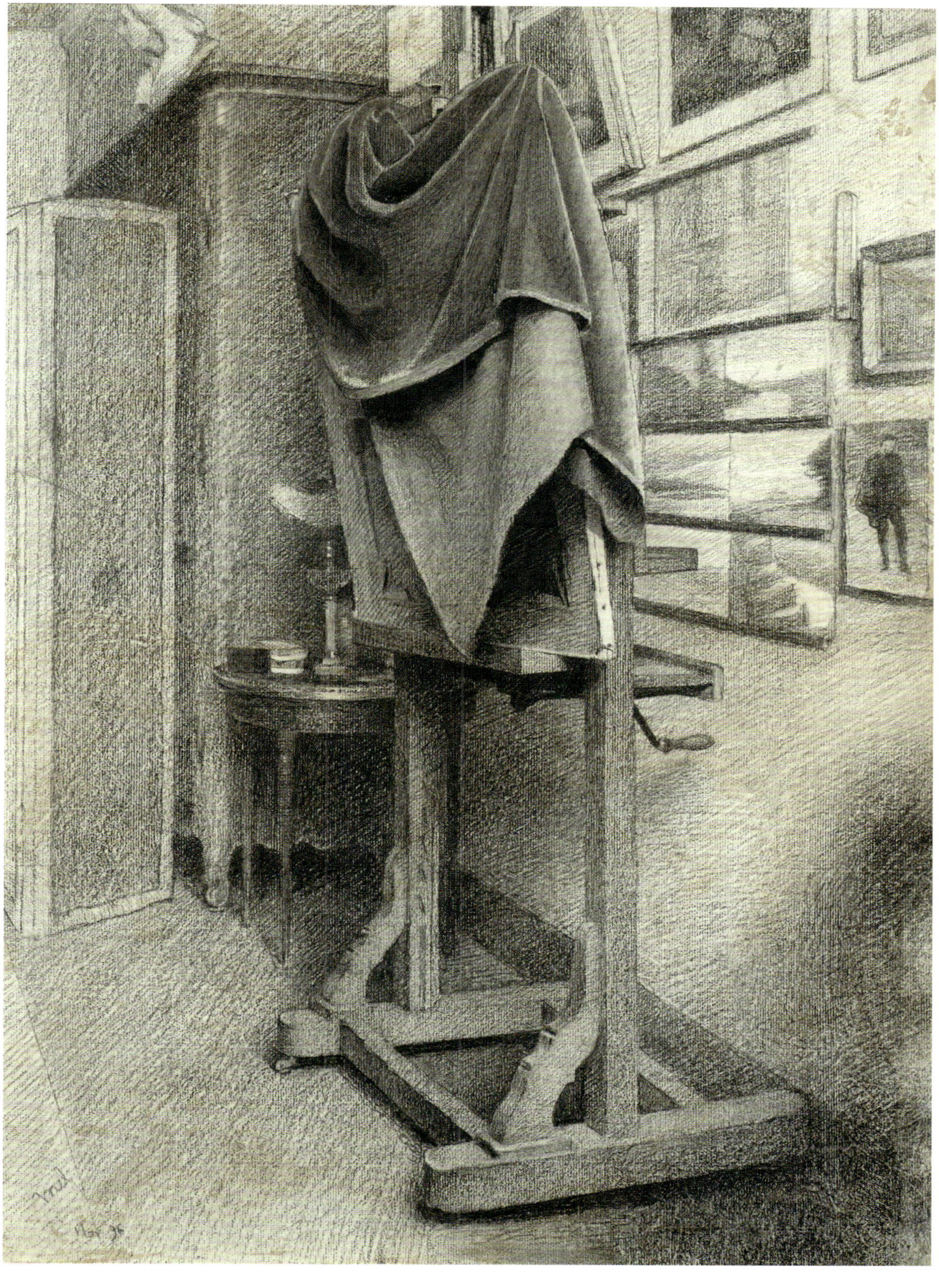

9

HORST JANSSEN (Hamburg 1929–1995 Hamburg)

The atelier of the sculptor Remo Rossi, Locarno 1972

Graphite and coloured chalks (white, red, yellow and green), 225 × 365 mm
Katrin Bellinger collection, inv. no. 1994-001

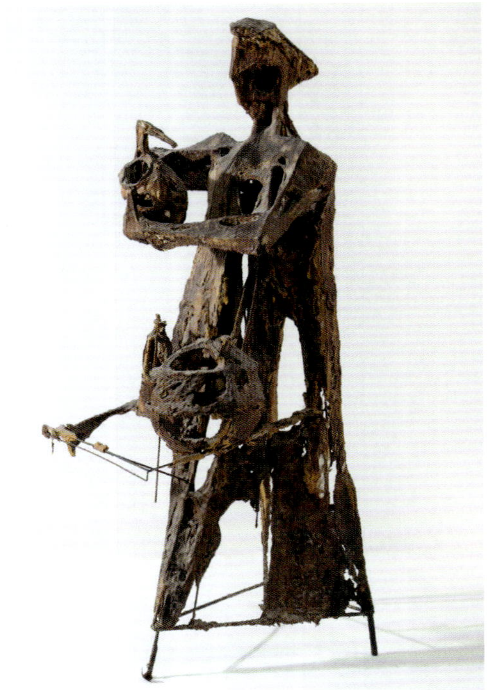

FIG. 16
Remo Rossi, *La Chimica*, 1964, iron and wax, 217 × 94 × 92 cm, Fondazione Remo Rossi, Locarno

This depiction of a sculptor's atelier belongs to a group of drawings, sharing the same format and technique, produced by Horst Janssen in the summer of 1972.[1] Dated and often inscribed, the sheets of what once was a sketchbook mainly depict the landscapes encountered by Janssen while travelling across Switzerland and Italy. This representation of an artist's studio stands out from the group and is a rare occurrence within Janssen's oeuvre as a whole. Though it has long remained unrecognised, we were able to identify it as the studio of the sculptor Remo Rossi (1909–1982) in Locarno. Janssen visited Locarno in 1972, during a trip with his friend the potter Gudrun Müller, but the drawing is currently the only evidence of Janssen's acquaintance with Rossi.

Remo Rossi was a prominent figure in Swiss art; from 1959 he created a cluster of ateliers surrounding his studio in Locarno. International artists such as Jean Arp, Hans Richter and Müller enjoyed Rossi's hospitality. The standing figure on the left is *La Chimica* (Chemistry) (fig. 16),[2] while the central female figure recalls the bronze *Donna incinta* (Pregnant woman), 1954, shown from behind.[3] The imposing scale of Rossi's statues combined with their enigmatic appearance would have appealed to Janssen's own taste for grotesque and unsettling images. The obscure personification of Chemistry, and Rossi's other works, silhouetted against the dark background, have become the studio's ghostly inhabitants. Typical of Janssen's spirited drawing style, this sheet combines an extensive use of graphite with touches of coloured chalks to convey specific chromatic passages, as with *La Chimica*, characterised by the rusty red of its wax coating.

INSCRIPTIONS Dated and located, lower right, *9.6.72 | Locarno b. Remo,* and monogrammed, *HJ*

PROVENANCE Thomas Le Claire Kunsthandel, Hamburg, 1994, from whom acquired

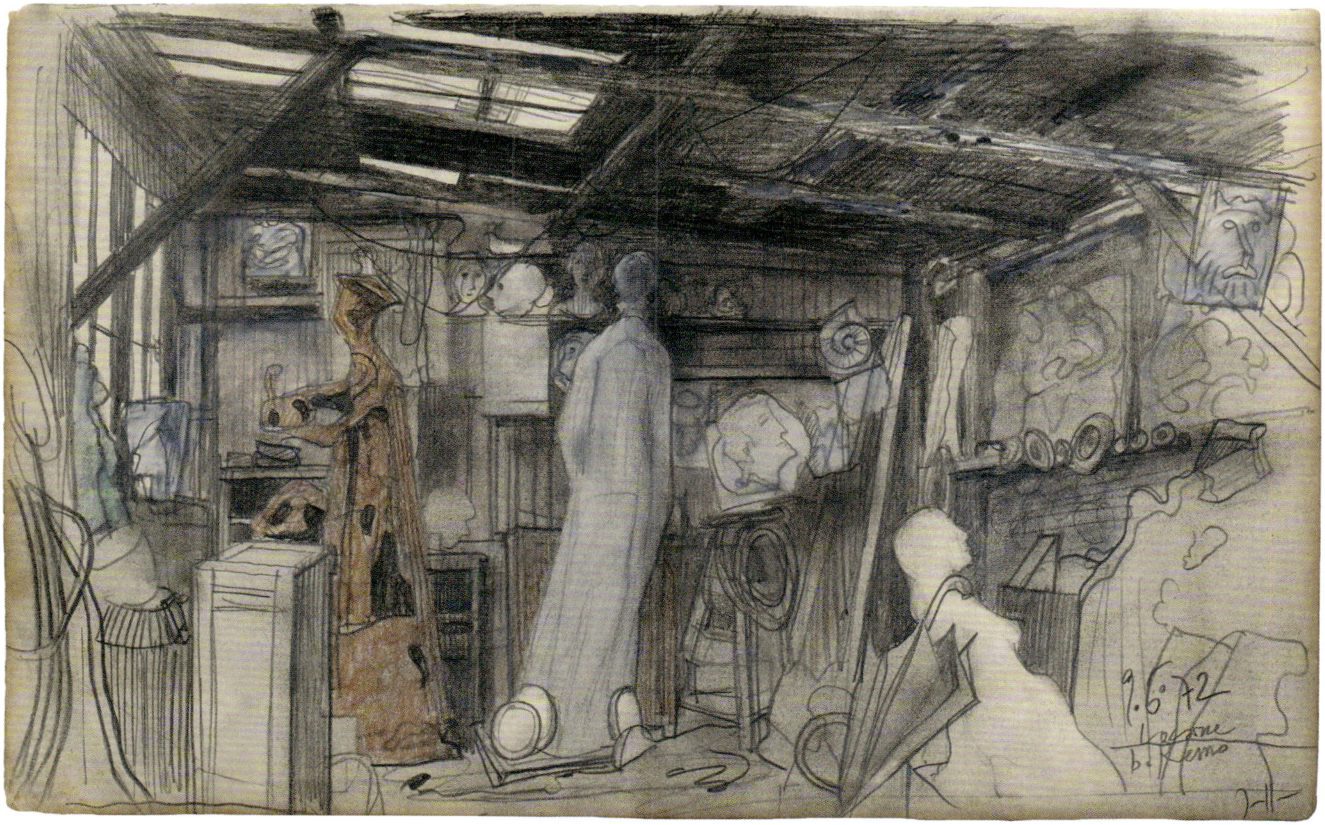
9.6.72

10

GEORGE GROSZ (Berlin 1893–1959 Berlin)

'Gute Zeit' (*Good Times*) 1940

Pen and black ink, watercolour, white heightening, 635 × 480 mm
Katrin Bellinger collection, inv. no. 2017-029

A successful and outspoken caricaturist and satirist, George Grosz became a prominent figure in Berlin's cultural milieu in the 1910s and 1920s. Because of his strong opposition to the rise of the Nazi regime, he was forced to leave Germany in 1933, and spent the rest of his career as an émigré artist. In 1938 Grosz became a naturalised American citizen and only returned permanently to Berlin in May 1959, where he died not long after. Apocalyptic landscapes and scenes of war recur in his works made in America, prefiguring the catastrophe that, years later, was to befall Europe. One such arresting work is the present self-portrait, ironically titled *Good Times*.[1]

The artist sits at his desk, fully concentrated on drawing with a reed pen, casually smoking his pipe. In his left hand he clutches three more pens, a cloth and an ink pot. Next to him, a pile of utensils is graphically delineated with confidence and speed. Only a few thin lines indicate the edges of the desk so that the artist and his objects appear to be floating on the white expanse of the large sheet. All around him, a desolate landscape unfolds: a bird of prey with spread wings holds a rat in its beak, a snake creeps up from under the table while beetles crawl upon the surface. In the background, a veiled sun looms over the scene. The mood is one of suspended threat. Datable to 1940, this work stands as a powerful and intimate expression of Grosz's concerns regarding the war and the events unfolding in his motherland. Around the same time as making the present drawing, he also dealt with the subject in a painting, dated 1940 (fig. 17).[2] Although both works share the same main elements, they differ in some respects. In the painting, Grosz looks out at the viewer, his gaze reading as a warning of the vision of impending danger that surrounds him.

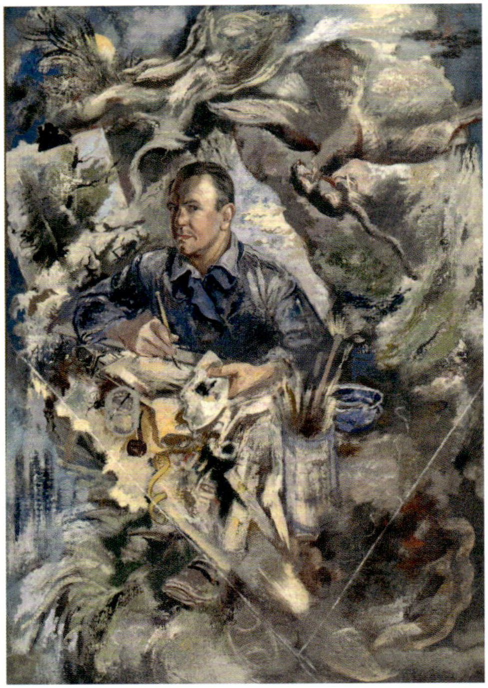

FIG. 17
George Grosz, *Self-portrait with bird of prey and rat*, 1940, oil on canvas, 118 × 83.5 cm
George Grosz Estate, 1959

INSCRIPTIONS Signed, lower left, in graphite, *Grosz*; verso numbered, *297*, and stamped, *4 13 8*

PROVENANCE De Vuyst, Lokeren, Belgium, 22 October 2016, lot 297; Galerie Bassenge, Berlin, 27 May 2017, lot 8078, from whom acquired

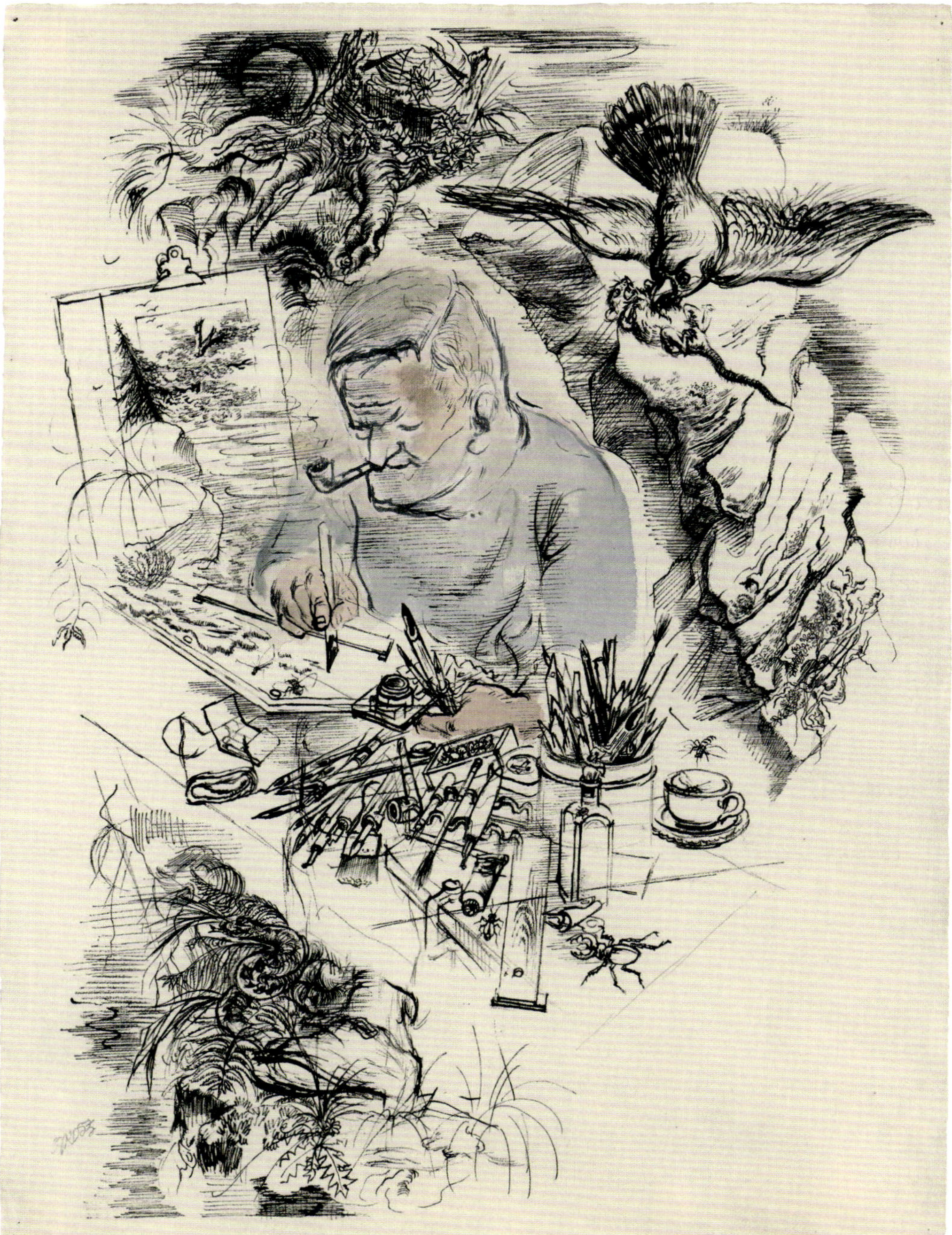

11

ERMENEGILDO ANTONIO DONADINI (Split 1847–1936 Radebeul)

The artist's studio, Munich 1877

Graphite, 348 × 417 mm
Katrin Bellinger collection, inv. no. 2010-011

Born in Split, Dalmatia, Ermenegildo Donadini initially trained in Vienna. He subsequently settled in Munich where he was master pupil of Carl Theodor von Piloty (1826–1886), a prominent genre and history painter at the Munich Academy.

This drawing of the artist's studio is dated 1877, thus at the end of Donadini's nearly five-year sojourn in Munich. It shows a sumptuously decorated interior filled with natural and manufactured objects. Perched on a small shelf, the statuette of a man with his right arm raised is a reproduction of Jean-Antoine Houdon's famous *Écorché* (Flayed man) of 1767, commonly used in the teaching of anatomy.[1]

The most prominent element of the composition is a fully dressed life-size mannequin, seated on a box or crate, with arms akimbo. This mannequin *d'atelier* would look quite convincing as a seated figure, were it not for its curled-up feet and lack of a head.[2] Representations of artists' studios often toy with the idea of the absent artist. Here, we may imagine him intent on arranging the mannequin in its desired position and fixing its garments – on a small table to the left lies what may be a piece of fabric, possibly part of the mannequin's voluminous sleeves.

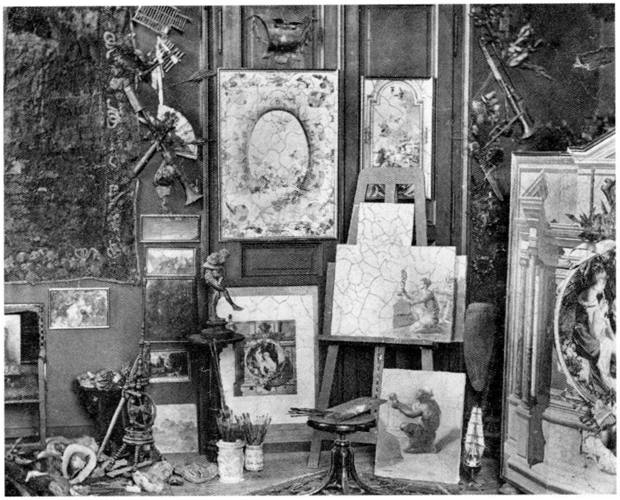

FIG. 18
Ermenegildo Antonio Donadini,
Donadini's Atelier, Vienna, 1878

Donadini's own photograph of his later atelier in Vienna (fig. 18) shows a cluttered studio interior similar to the one in the present drawing, and we may even recognise some of the same objects, such as the heraldic display of musical instruments which hangs on the wall to the right of the mannequin.[3]

INSCRIPTIONS Located, dated, signed and inscribed by the artist, lower right, *Monaco 12/1 1877. / EDonadini / Mio atelier*

PROVENANCE Ralph R. Haugwitz, Berlin, 2010, from whom acquired

EXHIBITIONS *Silent Partners: Artist and Mannequin from Function to Fetish*, Fitzwilliam Museum, Cambridge, 2014, no. c. 2

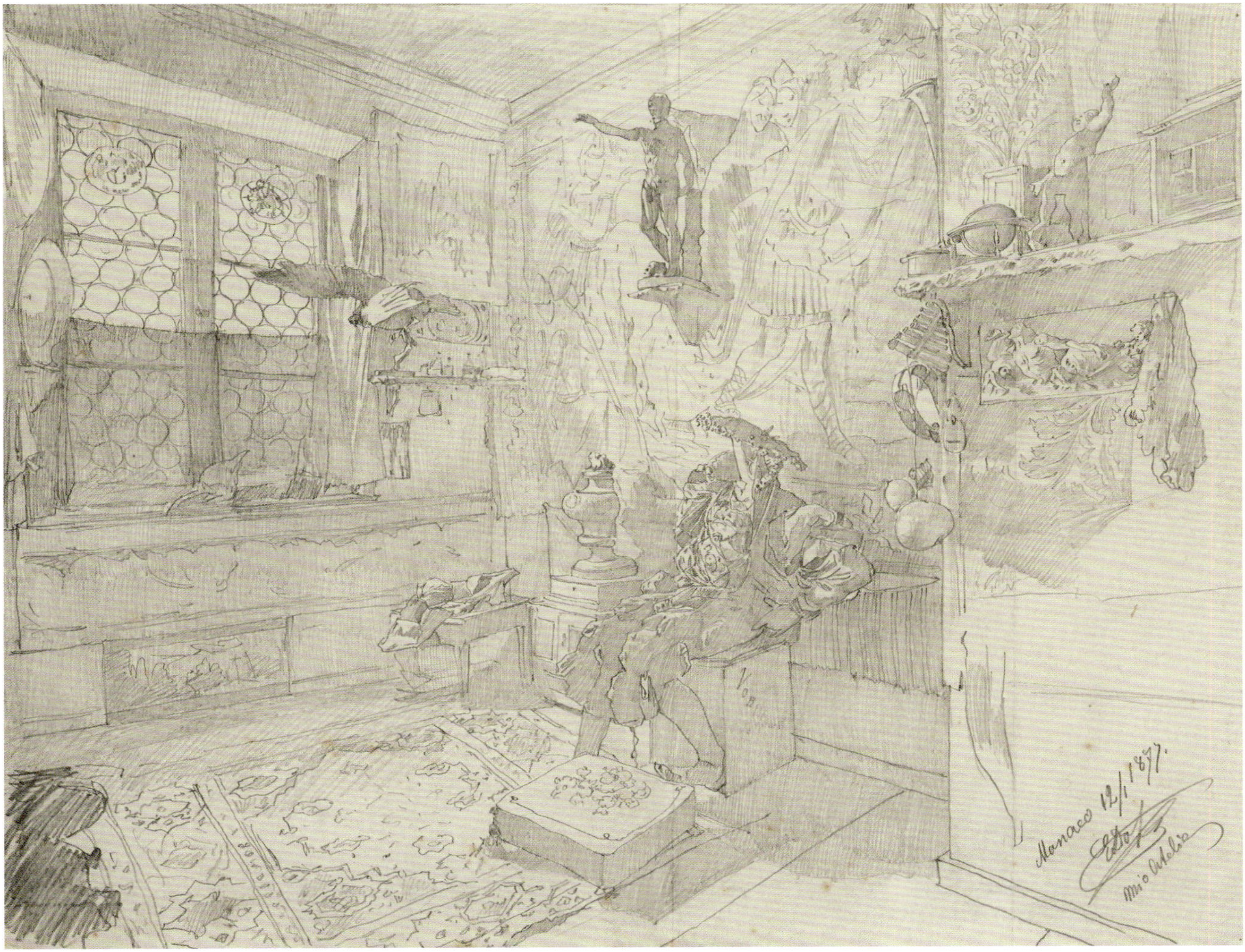
Monaco 12/1 1877.
Mio Atelier

12

JAMES ENSOR (Ostend 1860–1949 Ostend)

View of the artist's studio 1882

Black chalk, 224 × 175 mm
Katrin Bellinger collection, inv. no. 2013-006

The Belgian artist James Ensor began his training in his native coastal city of Ostend before attending the Académie Royale des Beaux-Arts in Brussels (1877–80). In 1880 he returned to Ostend and moved back into his family home. It was there, in the studio he set up for himself in the attic, that, until the mid-1880s, he filled several sketchbooks with black-chalk sketches of the house, his family (particularly his mother and sister), scenes of everyday life observed from his window, and his working space and the many objects inhabiting it. This vigorously rendered still life once belonged to one such sketchbook. Behind the table piled with drawings and art materials (canvases, bottles, sheets of paper), we catch a glimpse of Ensor's early painting *A colourist* (1880), portraying his sister Marie, herself an artist, intent on painting a fan.[1]

Although many of the motifs explored in the sketchbooks recur in his paintings, these drawings were not conceived as preparatory for more finished works, but, instead, document Ensor's exploration of the play of light on different textures and surfaces, as well as of the act of drawing itself. It was probably long after having made them that he cut the best drawings out of the sketchbooks, signed and dated them, and sold them to collectors. The several hundred sheets he did not sell remained in his family's possession and are today in the Royal Museum, Antwerp, which holds the largest collection of Ensor's works in Europe.[2]

INSCRIPTIONS Signed and dated, lower right, *Ensor 82*

PROVENANCE Libreria Antiquaria Prandi, Reggio nell'Emilia, 1976; private collection, Italy; Boquet & Marty de Cambiaire Fine Art, Paris, 2013, from whom acquired

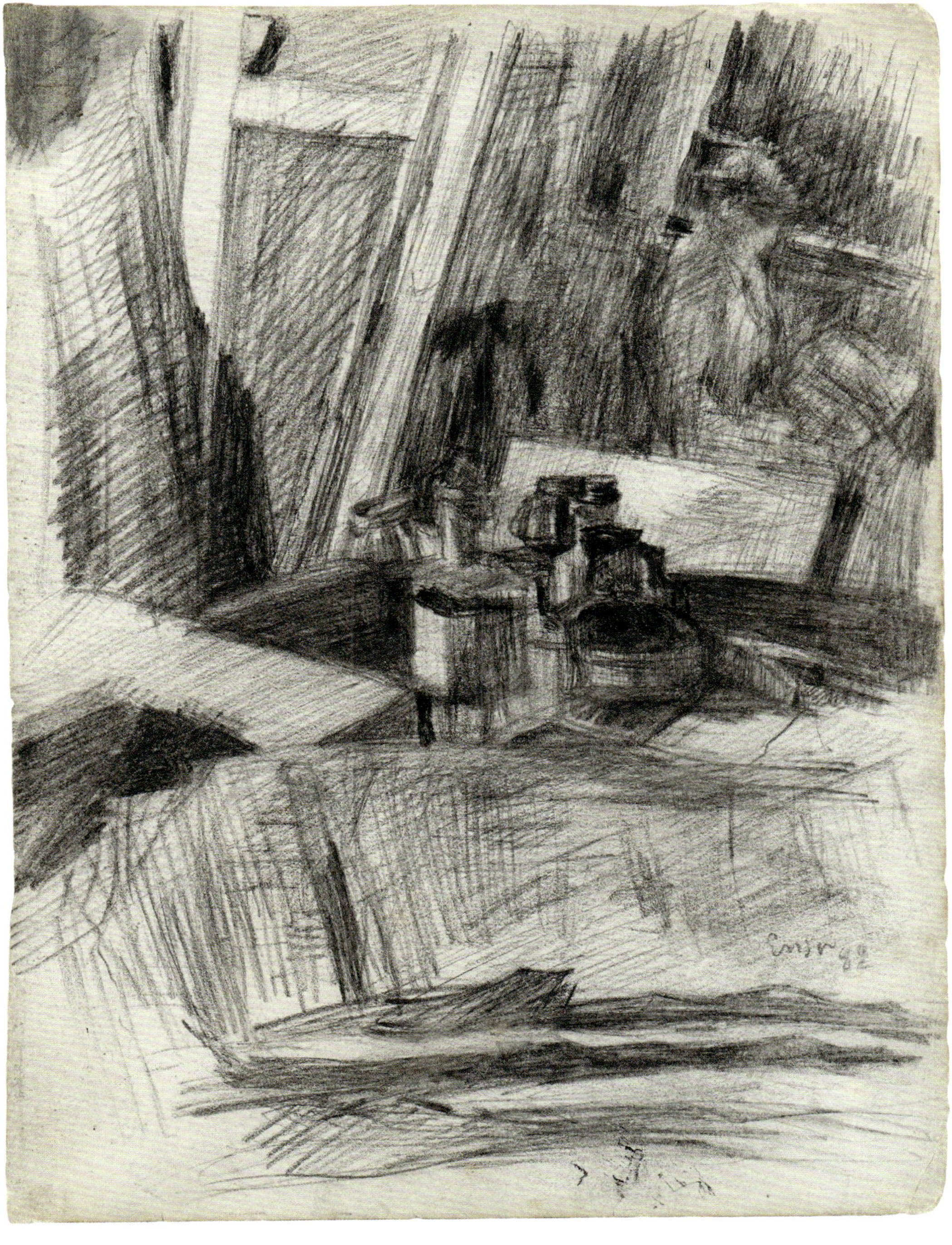

13

ADOLPH VON MENZEL (Breslau 1815–1905 Berlin)

Studies of a man painting 1888

Graphite with stumping, 200 × 125 mm
Katrin Bellinger collection, inv. no. 2011-022

A prolific and committed draughtsman, Adolph von Menzel would always carry multiple pocket-sketchbooks with him, so that thousands of his sketches survive today. Following a brilliant career as a painter – he was the most successful artist of his generation in Germany – from the late 1880s Menzel gave up oil painting to focus on gouache and drawing. His sketches of everyday subjects, encountered in the streets and restaurants of Berlin, show men and women deeply absorbed in their actions. As well as by people's physiognomies and attire, the artist's attention was also captured on occasion by working craftsmen and their tools.[1]

In this drawing, taken from life, a painter at work is shown in two different positions. At the top, he is observed frontally, leaning forward, painting with his right hand and holding a beer tankard, used as a paint can, in his left. Menzel has energetically scribbled out this figure's right arm, redrawing it beneath, with close attention to modelling and shading. The man occupying the lower part of the sheet is seen in profile, his features more clearly legible. In both studies, the painter's focused gaze and posture attest to his full engagement with the task at hand. Typical of Menzel's drawings from the late 1880s, this work may have been executed with a carpenter's pencil, which he favoured because of the wide range of tones it afforded, from deep velvety black to soft grey obtained by stumping.[2] These studies were used, with variations, as the starting point for the figure of a house painter working on a bannister on the upper right of Menzel's gouache *Beati possidentes* (Happy owners), 1888.[3]

INSCRIPTIONS Monogramed and dated, left margin, *A.M.* / *88*

PROVENANCE Schlumberger collection; Galerie De Bayser, Paris, 2011, from whom acquired

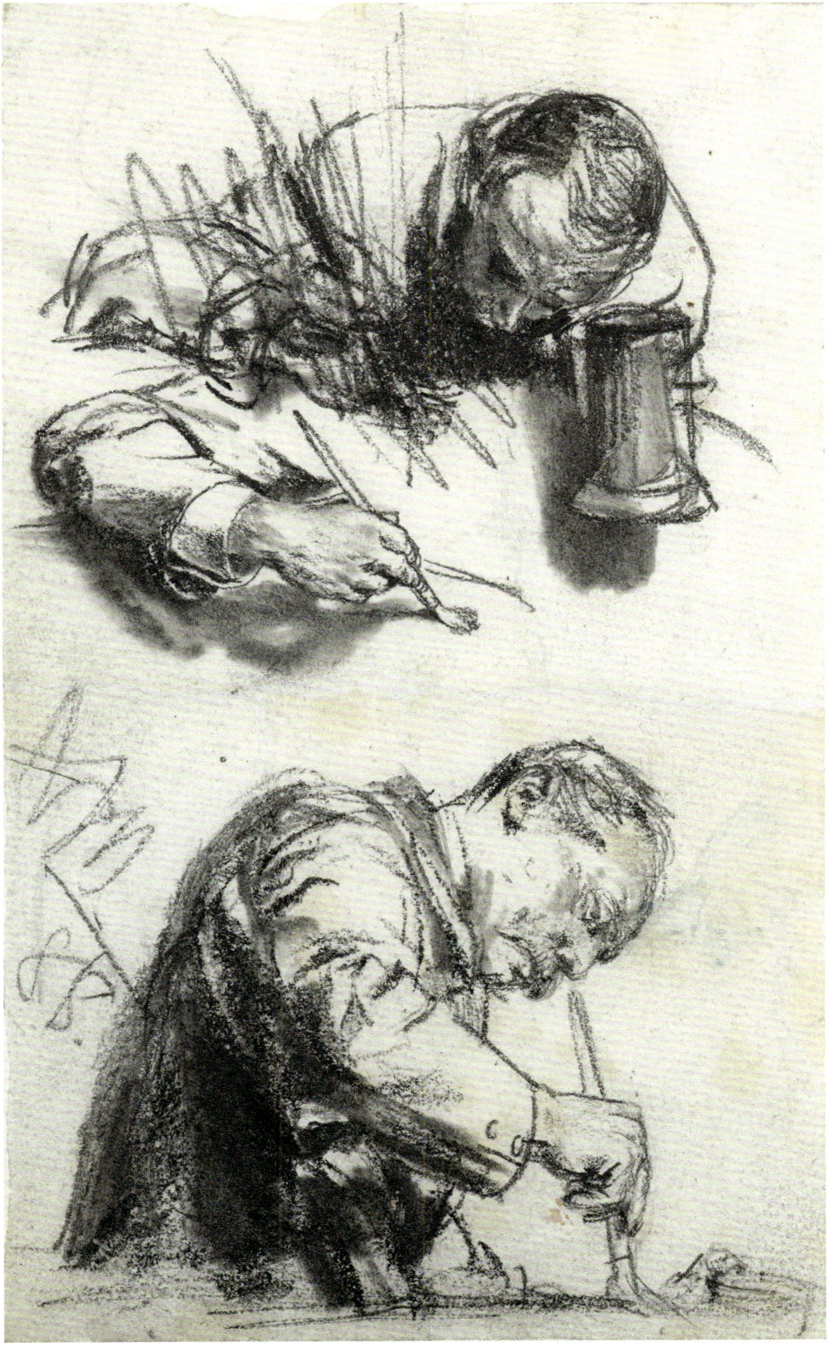

14

JULES DE GONCOURT (Paris 1830–1870 Paris)

Portrait of Mademoiselle Blanche Passy at an easel, wearing a man's cravat 1859

Graphite, 248 × 165 mm
Katrin Bellinger collection, inv. no. 2011-063

With her arched eyebrow and tightly pursed lips, the woman in this drawing appears fully absorbed in her work at the easel. However, her expression and her barely sketched brush-wielding right hand contrast with her exuberant outfit, utterly impractical for the act of painting. A large crinoline is surmounted by a cascade of petticoats, on top of which she wears an overdress which has been turned back as a precaution, so as to avoid any paint splashing on it. Flowers and leaves are arranged in her gathered dark hair. Around her neck, she wears a black cravat tied in a bow.

This absorbed figure of a female artist at work is a known individual; as the inscription at top left reveals, the model was Blanche Passy. The artist, Jules de Goncourt, fell in love with Blanche, sister of his childhood friend Louis Passy (1830–1913), who came from a family of financiers and economists. Their family retreat was at Gisors and the portrait was executed during one of Jules's stays there between 6 and 24 September 1859. While a potential marriage between Jules and Blanche may have been opposed by her family, she would nonetheless play a role in Jules's art. Blanche is in fact said to have been the primary inspiration behind the character of Renée Mauperin, protagonist of the eponymous novel written by Jules and his brother Edmond, first published in 1864. A modern, emancipated young lady, educated in the artistic culture of the nineteenth century, Renée prefers to paint in oil instead of watercolour, as convention dictated for women.[1] At one point in the novel she is described as wearing a black cravat made from a ribbon (*'une cravate faite d'un ruban noir'*),[2] just like Blanche in this drawing.

Mostly known for his literary association with Edmond, Jules was also a talented draughtsman and printmaker. He produced several copies of the large ensemble of drawings that he collected with his brother, to which a few original inventions can be added. One such work is this portrait of Blanche, which Jules gave to her as a gift, but of which he retained a copy (now in the archives of the Académie Goncourt, Paris). Jules's wish to be able to refer back to the drawing may be explained by its function: it helped him visualise the character of Renée Mauperin.[3]

INSCRIPTIONS Inscribed by the artist, upper left, *Blanche Passy*; located, dated and monogrammed, lower left, *Gisors 19 Sept. 59 / J. G.*

PROVENANCE Offered by the artist to Blanche Passy during a stay at the country retreat of the Passy family near Gisors; Tajan, Paris, 26 November 1999, lot 144; François Borne, Cheltenham, Gloucestershire, 2011, from whom acquired

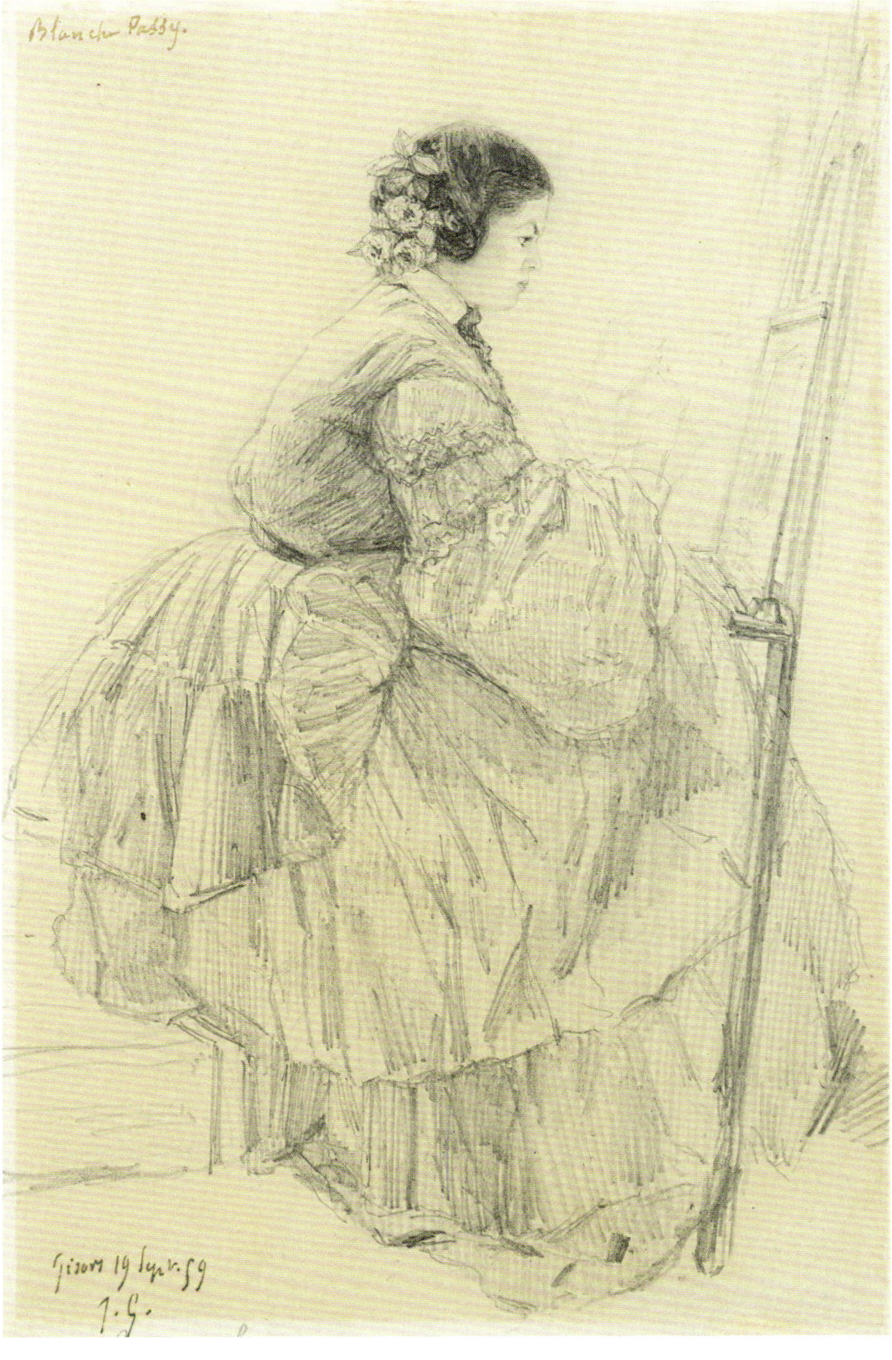
Blanche Passy.
Gisors 19 Sept. 59
J.G.

15

JEAN-AUGUSTE-DOMINIQUE INGRES (Montauban 1780–1867 Paris)

Portrait of the engraver Auguste-Gaspard-Louis Boucher-Desnoyers 1825

Graphite, 357 × 270 mm
Katrin Bellinger collection, inv. no. 1995-038

Although he aspired to be celebrated as a history painter, the French Neoclassical artist Jean-August-Dominique Ingres came to be primarily recognised as an excellent portraitist. His vast production includes several works immortalising his fellow artists. Ingres's graphite drawings are characterised by a great simplicity of composition and carefully chosen details. The sitter in this exquisite portrait is Auguste-Gaspard-Louis Boucher-Desnoyers (1779–1857), a prominent French engraver particularly admired for his prints after Raphael. After a brief period of apprenticeship in the studio of Alexandre Tardieu (1756–1844), he soon began to receive prestigious commissions, enjoying the favours of Napoleon and his court. He became a member of the Académie des Beaux-Arts in 1816 and in 1825, the year of Ingres's portrait, Desnoyers was appointed Engraver to the King, Charles X (ruled 1824–30). In 1828, he was created a baron.

In 1825, when he was himself elected a member of the Académie, Ingres executed three engravers' portraits. Aside from Desnoyers, the others were François Forster (1790–1872) and Tardieu.[1] While all three likenesses share an air of informality, resulting at least in part from the familiarity between artist and sitter, Desnoyers is the only one to be shown at work. He sits casually at his workbench, his tools at the ready, turned at three-quarters, with his face almost in frontal view. Gazing out towards the viewer, he gently leans his head against his left hand. In his right, he holds a burin over the plate he is working on. This is his celebrated engraving after Raphael's *Saint Catherine of Alexandria* (National Gallery, London), the cartoon for which had been in the Louvre since 1671.[2] Desnoyers's preparatory drawing for the print, delicately delineated but clearly legible, is propped up by his desk. Displayed at the Salon in 1824, Desnoyers's *Saint Catherine* must have been a great source of pride.

While the extent of the two French artists' acquaintance is not known with certainty, it is interesting to note that Desnoyers distinguished his finest proofs with a stamp derived from a drawing *à l'antique* by Ingres.[3]

INSCRIPTIONS Signed and dated, lower right, *Ingres del. 1825;* an old label on the back of the drawing reads, *A mon cher petit fils je donne ce portrait de mon grand'père, le Baron J. Desnoyers, premier graveur du roi, dessiné par Ingres en 1825. Bellerive Juin 1918*

PROVENANCE Auguste-Gaspard-Louis Boucher-Desnoyers, and by descent to his family; Hazlitt, Gooden & Fox, London, 1995, from whom acquired

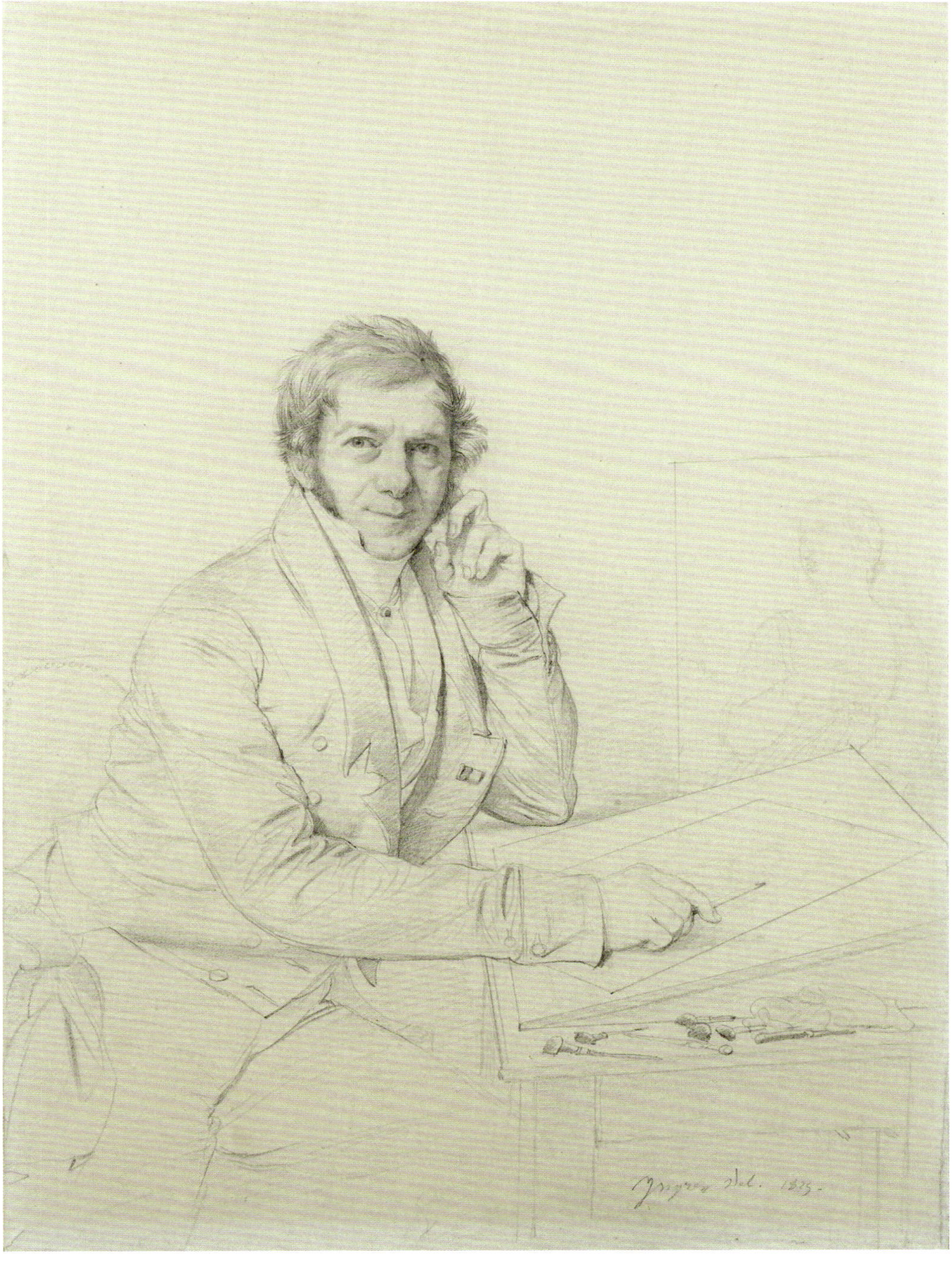
Ingres del.

16

FANNY GUILLAUME DE BASSONCOURT, BARONNE DE MOLARET (Chartres 1820–1888 Chartres?)

Portrait of an artist at her easel 1837

Graphite, 282 × 222 mm
Katrin Bellinger collection, inv. no. 2015-017

This elegant drawing shows a female artist working at her easel, seen from behind. Special emphasis is placed on the rendering of the sitter's elaborate hairstyle. Her long hair is gathered in a braided bun, held together by a comb. Soft curls fall on both sides of her face. Her dress has a large white collar and a ribbon-like belt around the waist. A decorative pattern is sketchily suggested on one of her petticoats. The artist paints with a fine brush, using a long mahl-stick to prevent her hand from touching the painted surface. A large palette, where several colours have been prepared, is balanced on her legs. She sits at an easel on to which two separate supports have been fixed. The top one is more legible and shows a landscape framed by a tree on the right-hand side, while a group of figures stand or sit at the centre. Recognisable by the faintly traced horizon line and tree branches, the lower work – the one that is currently being painted – corresponds to the sketch at the top. Thus, our artist may be working up in colour a composition she had previously sketched, perhaps *en plein air*.

To the right of the artist, a second easel and a stool topped by an open paint box complete the impression of looking over the artist's shoulder in her own work space. Little is known of Fanny, aside from her life dates and her maiden name, Guillaume de Bassoncourt. Interestingly, our sheet was once part of an album, now dismembered, which also included a drawing of a woman in the act of mending a bodice. The intimate nature of the scene suggests that Fanny may have used as models the women in her household, such as her mother and close friends.

INSCRIPTIONS Dated, lower right, *29 July 1837*

PROVENANCE Ralph R. Haugwitz, Berlin, 2015, from whom acquired

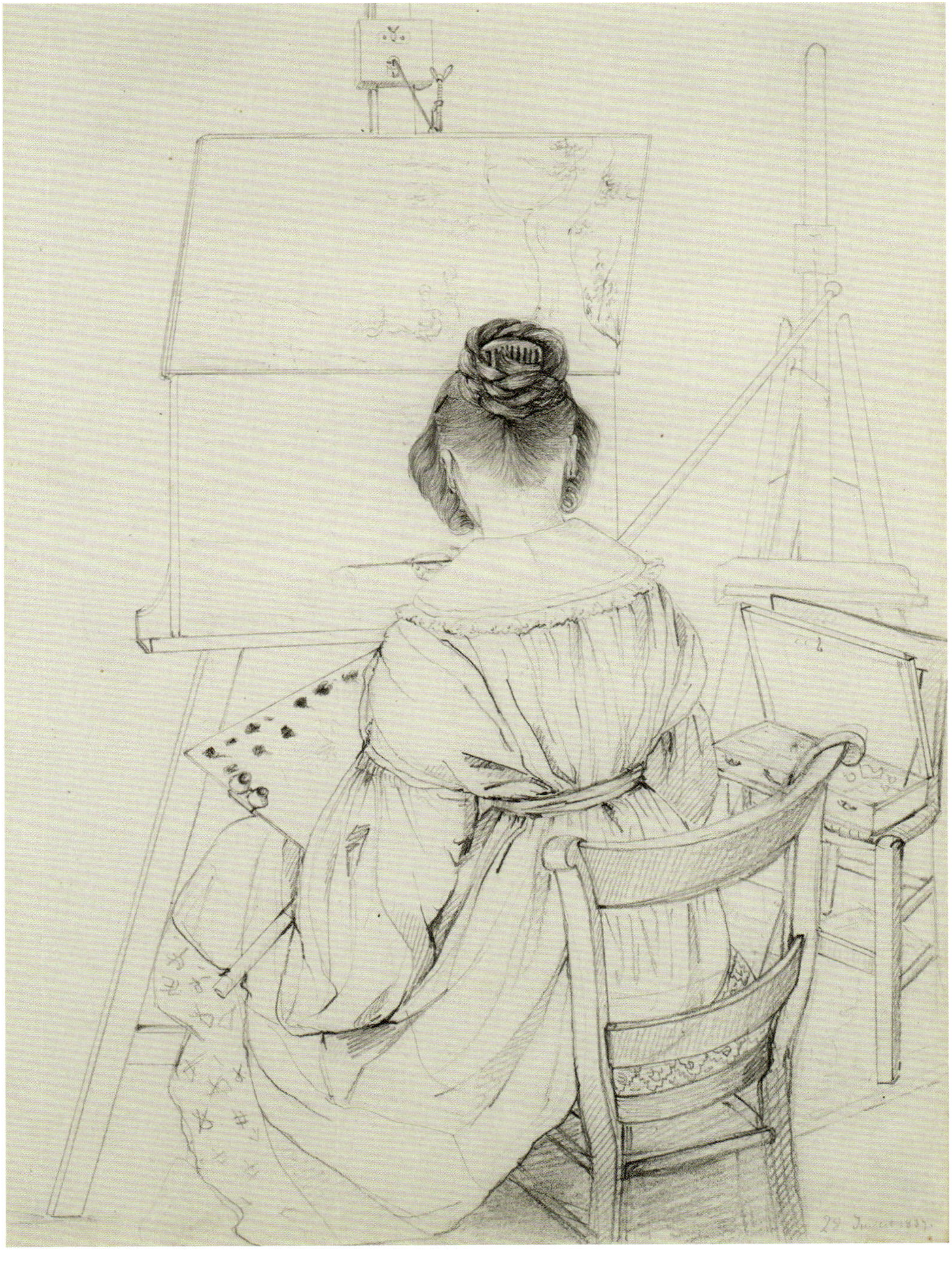

17

LOVIS CORINTH (Tapiau 1858–1925 Zandvoort)

Self-portrait with pencil and sketchbook 1924

Graphite, 313 × 248 mm
Katrin Bellinger collection, inv. no. 2017-006

Vigorously drawn in graphite, this is a captivating late self-portrait by the German artist Lovis Corinth. In it we see the artist studying his likeness in a mirror and simultaneously transferring it to his sketchbook. At once a record of his appearance and of the act of drawing it, this arresting image was executed just over a year prior to the artist's death, on 17 July 1925.

A prolific painter, printmaker and draughtsman, Corinth was a leading figure of the Berlin Secession. At the height of his artistic powers, in December 1911, he suffered a stroke that left him partially paralysed, drastically changing the course of his life. Not long before, in January 1911, Corinth had been chosen to succeed Max Liebermann (1847–1935) in the prestigious role of President of the Berlin Secession. Forced into a long period of recovery and rehabilitation, with the help of his wife, fellow painter Charlotte Berend (1880–1967), Corinth taught himself to draw and paint again.[1] His infirmity did not affect his productivity nor his creative drive – more than half of all his works date from 1912 to his death in 1925.

The new challenges posed by the consequence of his stroke fuelled Corinth's concerns with his own mortality and his predilection for self-analysis, which he explored both in his writings and in his works. In his numerous drawn, painted and etched self-portraits, many of which were made each year around his birthday (21 July), he reflected on his features and their changing over time. Compared to other late self-portraits, in the present drawing Corinth seems to have rendered his appearance with greater compassion.[2] The sense of urgency expressed by the insistent parallel hatching is balanced by the unconstrained *mise-en-page*, which allows the figure of the artist to inhabit the space of the sheet comfortably.

INSCRIPTIONS Signed and dated, upper left, *Lovis Corith / 12. Juni 1924.*

PROVENANCE Allan Frumkin, New York; Kornfeld, Bern, 16 June 2006, lot 45; private collection; Florian Härb, London, 2017, from whom acquired

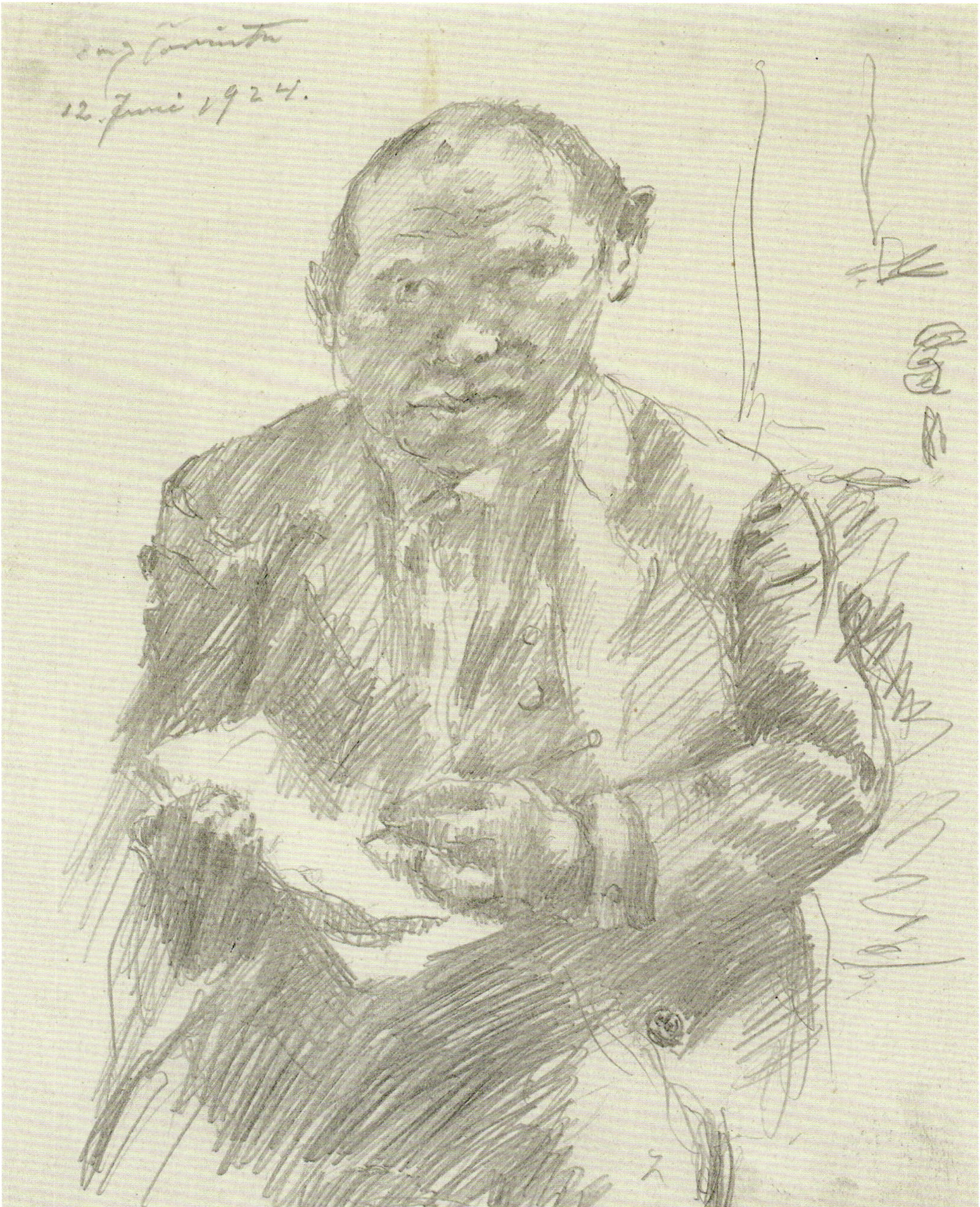
Lovis Corinth
12. Juni 1924.

18

HORST JANSSEN (Hamburg 1929–1995 Hamburg)

Don Quichotte =yolovi= [***I saw him***] (recto);
Study for the head of a child (verso, not illustrated) 1972

Graphite and brown chalk, 210 × 245 mm
Katrin Bellinger collection, inv. no. 2017-008

Throughout his prolific career, Horst Janssen experimented extensively with self-portraiture and creative copying, often with tantalising overlaps between the two. His approach to the Old Masters was not one of mere translation but involved instead a re-invention of his models. An indefatigable draughtsman, Janssen tended to use prints and drawings as models. His artists of choice included amongst others Michelangelo, Rembrandt, Claude Lorrain, Goya and Hokusai. In more than one instance he re-interpreted a work by Hyacinthe Rigaud (1659–1743), as in the case of the enigmatic *Don Quichotte =yolovi=*.

This extravagant invention is modelled on a drawing on blue paper where Rigaud placed a number of studies for a self-portrait (fig. 19).[1] With a few adjustments, Rigaud's hand topped by a palette, holding brushes and a mahl-stick, has turned into a face in profile surmounted by a large hat. Janssen's artist appears to be blinded by his strange hat, which arguably bears a resemblance to Don Quixote's helmet – in fact a basin, which, according to the character, was endowed with unique powers. The ironic similarity between the basin/helmet and a painter's palette was picked up by various artists before Janssen, and many more adopted the persona of Don Quixote as a metaphor for the artist himself.[2] The 'blind' artist may be unable to operate, or, conversely, he may be guided by his internal sight, his imaginative faculty. At once light-hearted and introspective, this drawing probably amused his fellow artist and friend Claus Clement, who also owned other drawings by Janssen.[3]

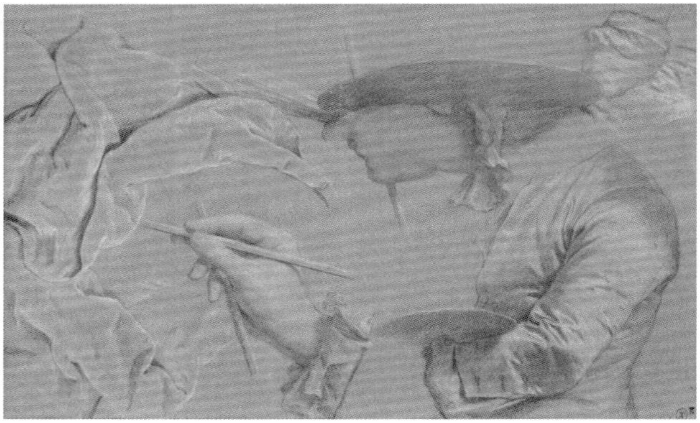

FIG. 19
Hyacinthe Rigaud, *Studies for a self-portrait*, c. 1730, black and white chalk, on blue paper, 284 × 459 mm, Wallraf-Richartz-Museum & Fondation Corboud, Graphische Sammlung, Köln, inv. no. 1961/026

INSCRIPTIONS Monogrammed and dated, lower right, *HJ* and *22.8.72*; titled, lower centre, *Don Quichotte =yolovi=*, and along lower right margin, *nach Hyacinthe Rigaud.*

PROVENANCE Claus Clement, Hamburg; Thomas Le Claire Kunsthandel, Hamburg, 2017, from whom acquired

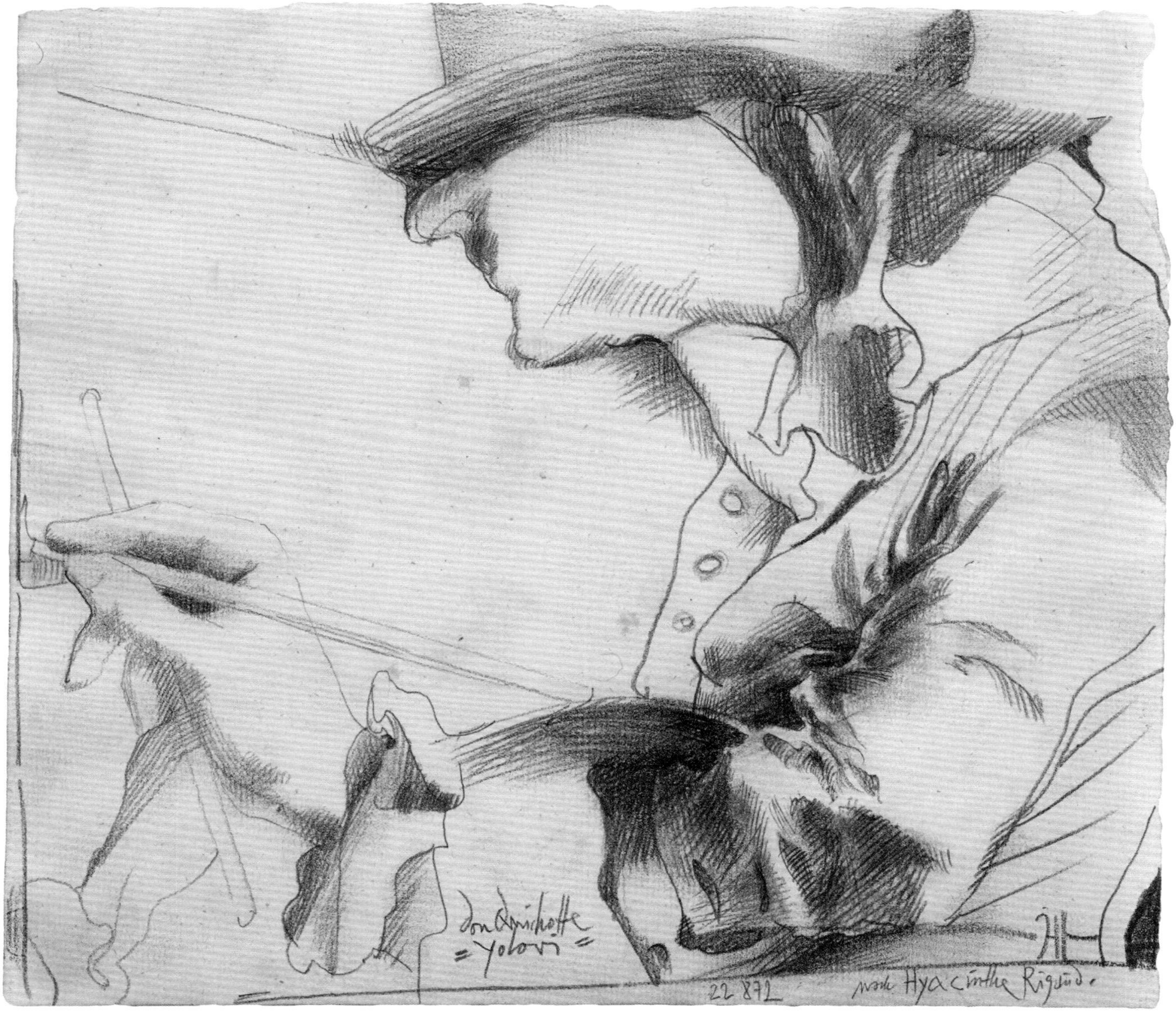

don Quichotte
=yolovi=
22 872
nach Hyacinthe Rigaud.

19

GIOVANNI DOMENICO TIEPOLO (Venice 1727–1804 Venice)

Punchinello as a portrait painter c. 1802–03

Black chalk, pen and brown ink, brown and ochre wash, 355 × 470 mm
Watermark: GA over F with a leaf-shaped cartouche surmounted by a fleur-de-lys
Katrin Bellinger collection, inv. no. 2004-014

This is one of a series of 104 highly finished drawings entitled *Divertimento per li regazzi* (Entertainments for children), executed by Domenico Tiepolo in the last years of his life and devoted to Punchinello, a popular character of the Commedia dell'Arte. For the scenes of the *Divertimento*, Domenico did not rely on any known text, but instead deliberately showcased his powers of invention.

One group of drawings shows Punchinello and his companions taking on a variety of professions, in this case that of portrait painter. Holding palette and brush, Punchinello sits at an easel, his gaze directed not at the work at hand but at his sitter, as if inspecting her appearance. There may be some discrepancy between the sitter and her likeness, since the standing hatless Punchinello, acting as the sitter's sponsor, extols some features the painter appears to have overlooked. This has caused a crowd to gather in the studio to see for themselves and pass judgement on the disputed portrait. A contemporary audience would have easily associated such a joke with Punchinello's antics in the Commedia dell'Arte.

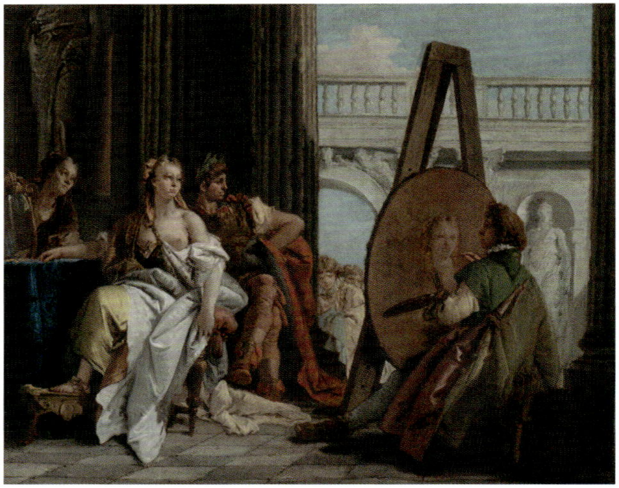

FIG. 20
Giovanni Battista Tiepolo, *Alexander the Great and Campaspe in the studio of Apelles*, c. 1740, oil on canvas, 42.5 × 54 cm, The J. Paul Getty Museum, Los Angeles

INSCRIPTIONS Signed, lower left, *Dom°Tiepolo f.*, and numbered, upper left, 70 (altered from 79?)

PROVENANCE Private collection, London; anonymous sale, Sotheby's, London, 6 July 1920, part of lot 41 (among 102 'Carnival Scenes'); P.D. Colnaghi & Co., London, 1920; Richard Owen, Paris, 1920; Robert Goelet, New York; anonymous sale (Goelet?), Sotheby's, London, 6 July 1967, lot 38; Seiferheld Galleries, New York; Alice M. Kaplan, New York; private collection; Hazlitt, Gooden & Fox, London, 2004, from whom acquired

SELECTED EXHIBITIONS *Drawings from New York Collections III: the Eighteenth Century in Italy*, The Metropolitan Museum of Art, New York, 1971, no. 279; *Domenico Tiepolo's Punchinello Drawings*, Indiana University of Art, Bloomington, 1979, no. 28; *The Glory of Venice: Art in the Eighteenth Century*, Royal Academy, London, 1995, no. 225

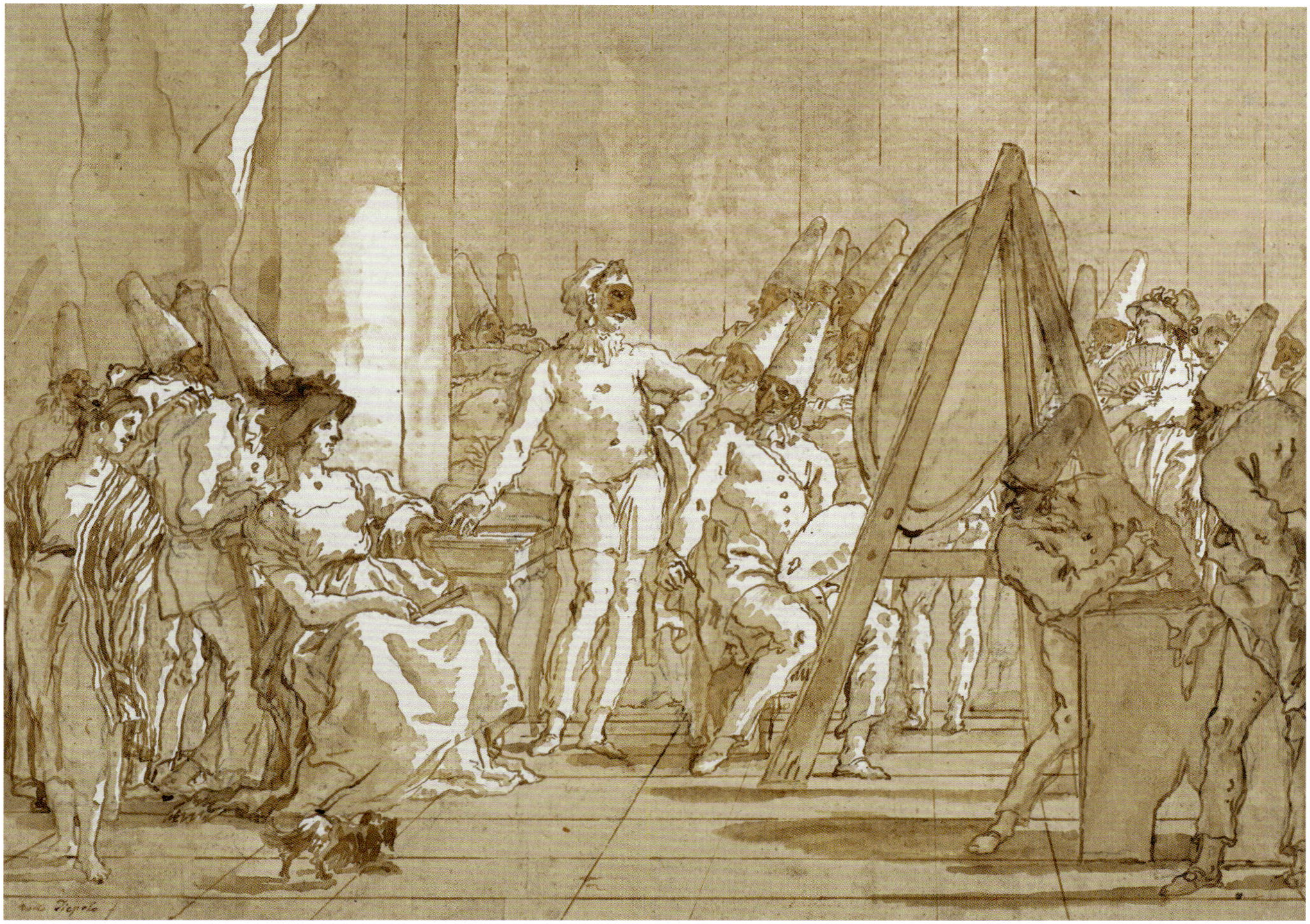

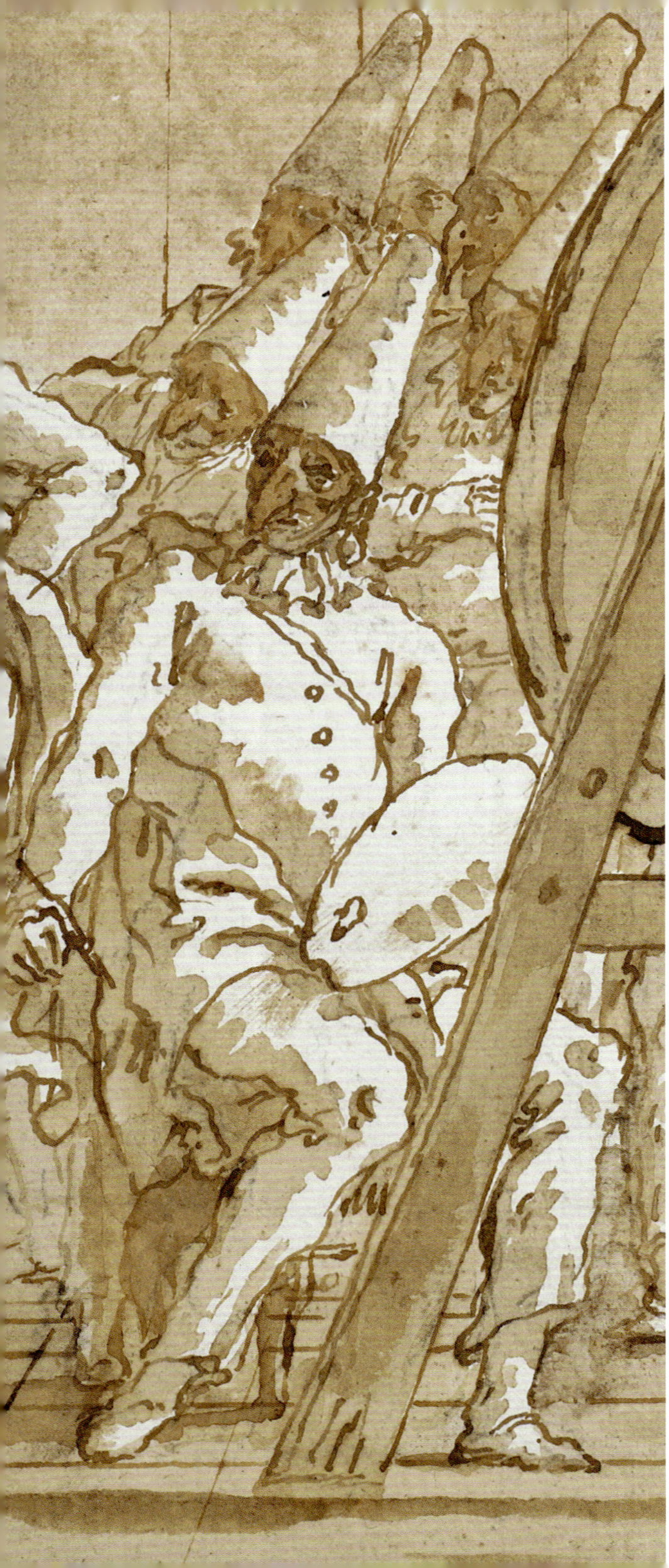

On one occasion, Punchinello even paints the wrong lady's portrait and then demands payment.[1] In the drawing, the comedic tone of the scene is increased by Domenico's decision to turn the canvas away from the viewer and to depict all those present, apart from the women, sporting Punchinello's conical hats, beaked masks and ruffle collared costumes.

The central trio of painter, sitter and sponsoring figure is loosely based on Domenico's father Giovanni Battista's painted versions of *Alexander and Campaspe in the studio of Apelles* (fig. 20).[2] According to Pliny the Elder's *Natural History* of AD 77, having been commissioned to paint a portrait of Alexander the Great's favourite concubine, Campaspe, the painter Apelles fell in love with his sitter while capturing her beauty on canvas. Such was Alexander's esteem for his court painter that he decided to keep the portrait – and hand Campaspe to Apelles! Domenico's invention thus subverted this tale, originally meant to celebrate the power and persuasiveness of painting, in order to offer a partly self-reflective parody of the painter's profession.

20

JEAN-HONORÉ FRAGONARD (Grasse 1732–1806 Paris)

The inspiration of the artist c. 1760–63

Black chalk, pen and brown ink, brown wash, brown ink framing lines, 230 × 349 mm
Katrin Bellinger collection, inv. no. 2017-025

An artist sits back in his chair, his right hand theatrically covering his eyes while in his left he holds a pencil or brush.[1] In front of him, on a table covered with a tasselled drapery, a folio propped up on two albums seems to hold a blank sheet of paper. The theme of artistic inspiration comes to the fore. All around the central figure, which can be read as a metaphorical self-portrait of Fragonard himself, various visions take shape, as if emerging directly from the artist's fertile imagination. At top right, we see a personification of Painting accompanied by putti; her pose and outspread wings are almost mirrored by those of the harpy that floats behind the desk. Other dreamlike motifs, which recur in Fragonard's paintings, are faintly delineated in the area above the central figure – a jester, a figure holding the head of a cow, a dove and an owl flying at the centre. A brooding cat at the very foreground may be a symbol of wisdom guiding the artist.

INSCRIPTIONS Inscribed on the mount, lower left, in pen and brown ink, *Fragonard*

PROVENANCE Count Antoine Seilern, London (1901–1978), by whom donated for a sale in aid of the Red Cross, Christie's, London, 2 October 1942, lot 34; Léon Genon, Brussels, then by descent; sale, Sotheby's, London, 6 July 2016, lot 231, at which acquired

EXHIBITIONS *Fragonard: Drawing Triumphant. Works from New York Collections*, New York, Metropolitan Museum of Art, 2016 (ex catalogue)

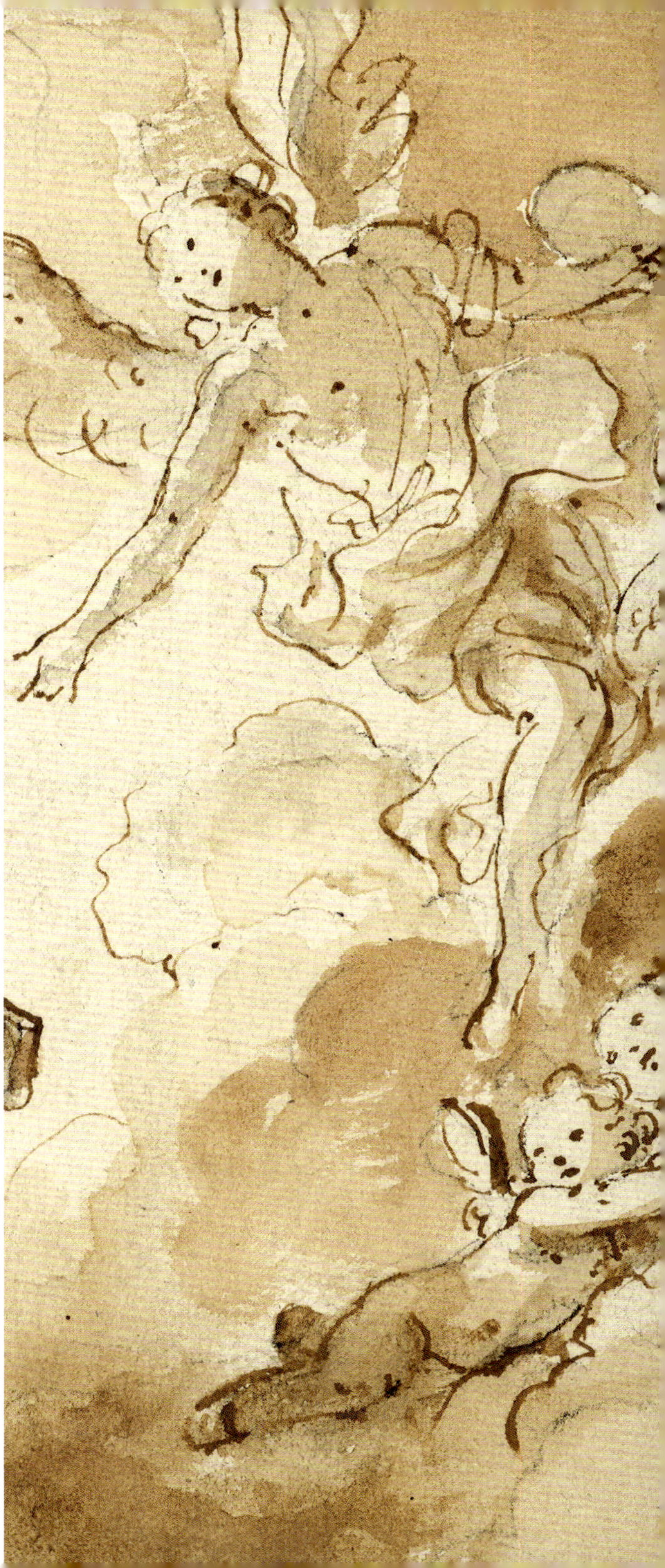

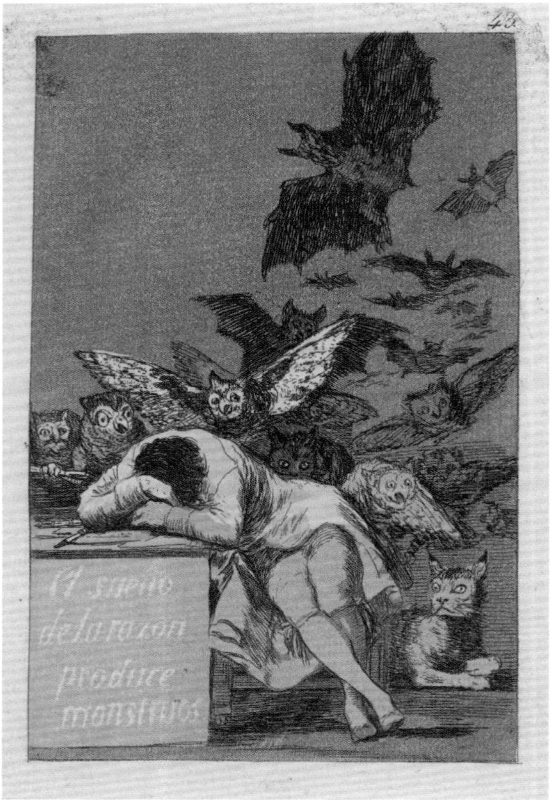

FIG. 21
Francisco de Goya, *El sueño de la razon produce monstruos* (The sleep of reason produces monsters), 1799, from *Los caprichos*, plate 43, etching and aquatint, 215 × 150 mm, The British Museum, London, inv. no. 1975,1025.124

The painterly application of wash emphasises the dream-like atmosphere permeating the scene. Stylistic considerations suggest a dating to the 1760s, prior to Fragonard's second trip to Italy in 1773–74. The drawing's themes also seem to accord with such a dating, as the artist was then assuming control of his career. Turning aside from the more traditional path of prestigious commissions that would have granted him access to the Académie royale, Fragonard would take a different route, catering to a select group of enlightened collectors. It was around this time, in fact, that he started working on his illustrations of Jean de La Fontaine's *Fables*, the first of his highly original series of drawings based on literary texts.[2]

Fragonard dealt with the topic of creative inspiration in other drawings made between the 1760s and the early 1780s, although never with such personal tones.[3] A compelling parallel can be drawn between the imagery of the present drawing and Goya's later *El sueño de la razon produce monstruos* (The sleep of reason produces monsters), from his series *Los caprichos* (fig. 21).[4] Both works share certain elements in their autobiographical depiction of the artist's imaginative power, somewhere between creative energy and torment.

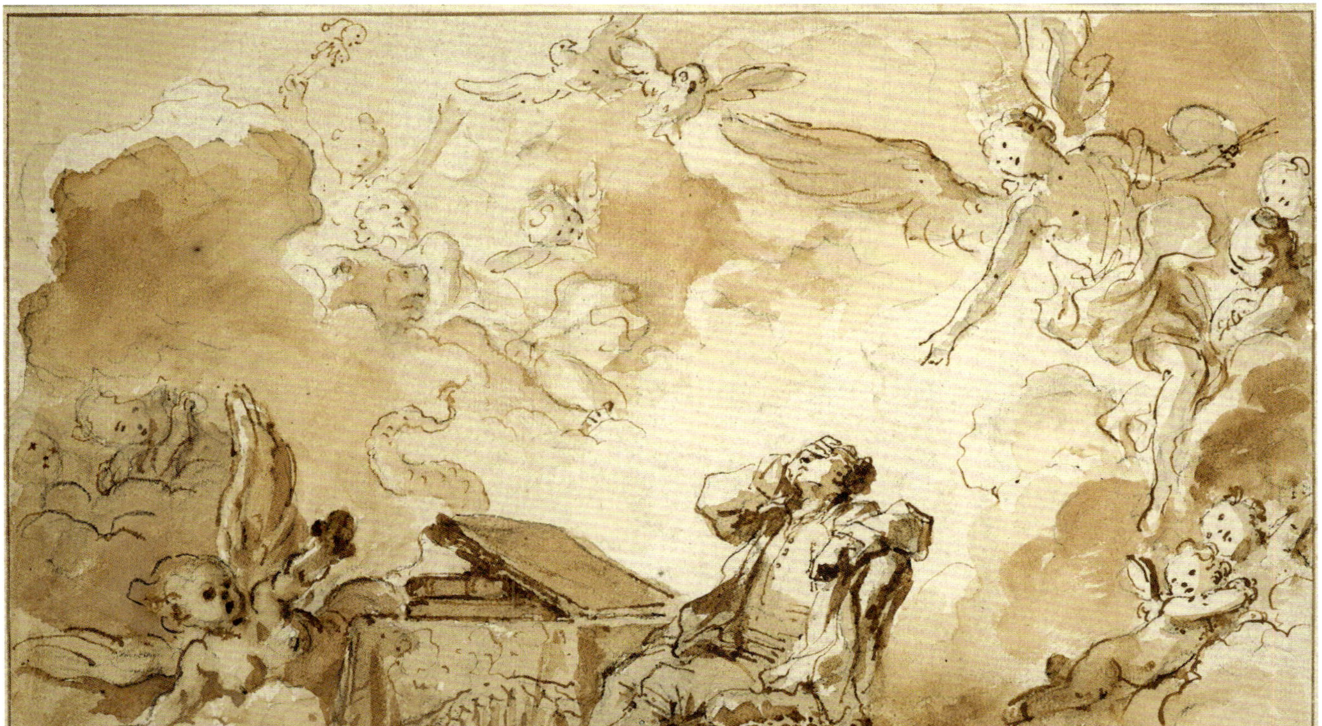

21

CORNELIS DUSART (Haarlem 1660–1704 Haarlem)

The old painter

Black chalk, pen and brown and black ink, grey wash, brown ink framing lines, 216 × 183 mm
The British Museum, London, inv. no. 1836,0811.131

This drawing shows an aged painter working at his easel within a studio interior filled with tools and art materials.[1] Instead of peering over the artist's shoulder, here we are confronted with his concentrated facial expression. Both his thick glasses and his contorted lips may hint at the old painter's unwavering commitment to the exercise of his profession. On a stool next to the easel, a pile of objects includes a violin. Disguised as a casual complement to the painter's possessions, just another studio prop, the violin may alert us to the scene's allegorical overtones. At top right on one of the back-wall shelves, a skull makes its appearance, a well-known reminder of the transitory nature of human life. Musical instruments are often included in Dutch *vanitas* still lifes in connection to the vanity of human endeavours. In addition, the violin, with its strings visualising the concept of physical and temporal continuity, alludes even more explicitly to the finite duration of human life. This may then be Cornelis Dusart's take on the Latin adage *ars longa, vita brevis* (art is long, life is short).

Dusart was a painter, draughtsman and printmaker active in Haarlem. A pupil of Adriaen van Ostade (1610–1685), he inherited his master's studio and re-worked several of his drawings, to render them more marketable. Van Ostade specialised in genre scenes featuring groups of peasants and families in humble domestic settings. On more than one occasion, he dealt with the theme of the artist at work, most notably in *The painter's studio*, c. 1670–75.[2] In a dark interior, an unpretentious landscape painter works at the easel; two apprentices go about performing their tasks in the background. Though not a self-portrait, van Ostade's scene reads as a self-reflective joke on his own specialisation; who better than this humble craftsman could paint his peasant scenes? The gentle humour of van Ostade's works finds parallels in Dusart's penchant for caricature and veiled parody. Stylistically close to the British Museum sheet, his own *Painter in the studio*, c. 1690, at the Rijksmuseum, is arguably an irreverent parody of the higher status granted to history painters.[3]

PROVENANCE John Sheepshanks (1787–1863); William Smith (1808–1876); purchased by the British Museum, 1836

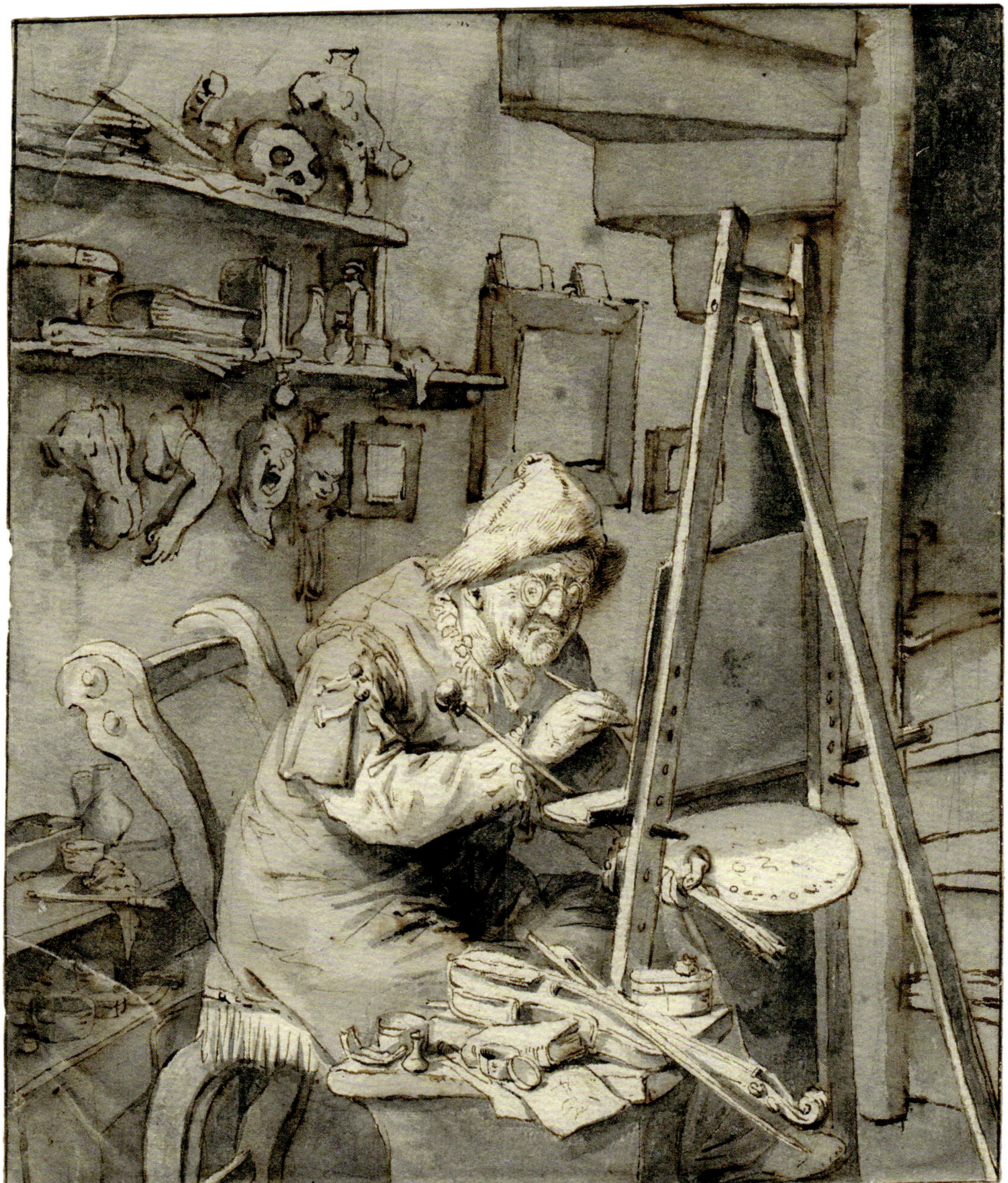

22

ATTRIBUTED TO DAVID KANDEL (active in Strasbourg 1520–92)

Virtue protecting the artist 1587

Pen and black ink, grey wash, 165 × 144 mm
Katrin Bellinger collection, inv. no. 1992-008

This drawing of *Virtue protecting the artist* was probably executed as an independent work of art, as a proclamation of ambition and artistic achievement. It shows Virtue, crowned with laurel and holding the palm of glory, in the act of shielding an artist from Envy. The man sits on a stone block, a tablet or sketchbook balanced on his right leg. Holding a quill in each hand, he draws a Venus-like statuette. Deeply absorbed in his activity, the draughtsman seems oblivious to the imposing winged figure towering over him. Virtue's nemesis, Envy, is symbolised through a stormy sky, with thunder and hail exploding from the clouds.

This exuberant drawing, elegantly monogrammed and dated, can be attributed to the sixteenth-century German printmaker David Kandel, active in Strasbourg. He is well-known for his animal prints in Sébastien Münster's *Cosmographia Universalis* (Basel, 1578), and for his numerous wood engravings in Hieronymus Bock's herbal, the *Kreutterbuch* (Strasbourg, 1546).[1] His prints are often signed with his monogram 'DK' enclosed within two tiny stars, or simply with the initial 'D'.

Drawings by Kandel are few and far between. Two portraits in pen and ink, both in the Musée du Louvre, are faintly inscribed with his interlaced monogram, and currently accepted as autograph. The first, a profile portrait of Hieronymus Bock holding a flower, was engraved by Kandel.[2] The second, a half-length portrait of a young boy in a hat holding a book – also used as the model for a print, although not by Kandel – shows the likeness of the Polish-Lithuanian prince Nicolas Christophe Radziwiłł (1549–1616).[3] Compared to the Louvre examples, *Virtue protecting the artist* is more finished and combines lines in pen and ink with delicate touches of grey wash applied with a brush, perhaps attesting to its conception as an independent work.

INSCRIPTIONS Monogrammed, lower right, *DK*, inscribed within the image, *VIRTVS*, and dated on the pedestal on the right, *1587*

PROVENANCE Arnoldi-Livie, Munich; private collection, from which acquired in 1992

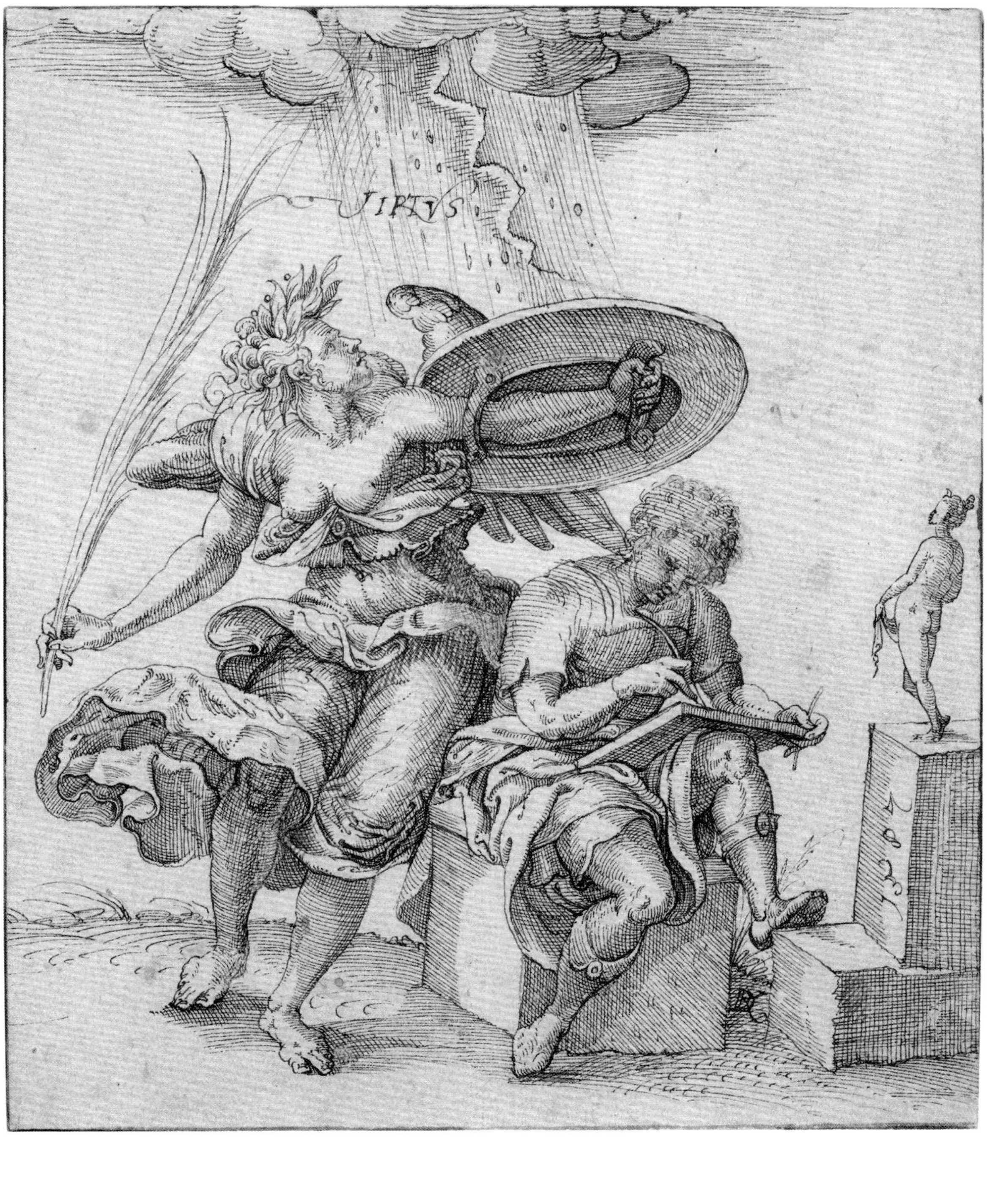
VIRTVS

NOTES

I would like to thank the following people for their support and advice: Christopher Boulden, Sarah Catala, Jamie Gabbarelli, Martin Grässle, Florian Härb, Ralph Haugwitz, Hinrich Sieveking and Giulia M. Weston
—ANITA VIOLA SGANZERLA

Cat. 1

1 See Konrad Oberhuber, 'Bruegel's Early Landscape Drawings', *Master Drawings*, 19 (1981), pp. 146–56, 206–19 (p. 149, pl. 23).

2 Cf. Nadine M. Orenstein, *Pieter Bruegel the Elder: Drawings and Prints* (exh. cat., The Metropolitan Museum of Art, New York, 2001), pp. 268–76, nos. 120–25.

Cat. 2

1 On Lambert Doomer's life see Wolfgang Schulz, 'Doomer and Savery', *Master Drawings*, 9 (1971), pp. 253–59, 316–31; Werner Sumowski, *Drawings of the Rembrandt School*, ed. and trans. by Walter L. Strauss, 10 vols. (New York: Abaris Books, 1979–92), II (1979), p. 783. Peter Schatborn ('Review of *Lambert Doomer, Sämtliche Zeichnungen*, by W. Schulz', *Simiolus* 9 (1977), 48–55 [p. 50]) questions Doomer's apprenticeship in Rembrandt's studio.

2 Sumowski, pp. 980–81, no. 458x.

3 Sumowski, pp. 860–61, no. 401.

4 Known from a later autograph replica of a drawing made by Doomer while travelling in c. 1663, now in the C. Croockewit-van Eeghen Collection, Arnhem; Sumowski, p. 1038, no. 486x.

Cat. 3

1 Ben Broos and Marijn Schapelhouman, *Nederlandse tekenaars geboren tussen 1600 en 1660* (Zwolle: Waanders, 1993), p. 51, no. 34, fig. b.

2 De Bisschop, *Two draughtsmen seated outdoors*, Amsterdam Museum, inv. no. A 18179; Huygens the Younger, *Two draughtsmen near Zorgvliet*, Municipal Archive of The Hague, Gr. A 110; illustrated in Aymonino and Lauder, *Drawn from the Antique*, p. 142, figs. 2–3.

3 Jan G. van Gelder and Ingrid Jost, *Jan de Bisschop and his Icones & Paradigmata: Classical Antiquities and Italian Drawings for Artistic Instruction in Seventeenth Century Holland*, 2 vols. (Doornspijk: Davaco, 1985).

Cat. 4

1 A very similar view is found in a drawing by Thomas Jones, dated 1778, private collection; cf. Ann Sumner and Greg Smith, eds., *Thomas Jones (1742–1803): An Artist Rediscovered* (exh. cat., National Museum & Gallery, Cardiff, 2003), p. 196, no. 89.

2 Czarskoje Selo, Pushkin, Palace of Catherine II, inv. no. ED-201-X; *Paysages d'Italie: les peintres du plein air* (1780–1830) (exh. cat., Galeries Nationales du Grand Palais, Paris, 2001), p. 7, no. 2.

Cat. 5

1 On Gehbe's life and work see Nikolaus Schaffer in *Allgemeines Künstlerlexikon. Die bildenden Künstler aller Zeiten und Völker*, ed. by Günter Meißner, vol. 52 (Munich: K. G. Saur Verlag, 2006), p. 26.

2 Cf. Gehbe's painting *Wald mit alter Mühle (Forest with old mill)*, c. 1883, Salzburg Museum, inv. no. 245–29.

3 Compare, for instance, Preller's sketchbook in the Graphische Sammlung Albertina, Vienna, inv. no. 25884.

Cat. 6

1 *Rome 1760–1770: Fragonard, Hubert Robert et leurs amis* (exh. cat., Galerie Cailleux, Paris, 1983), under no. 7.

2 Jean de Cayeux, *Les Hubert Robert de la Collection Veyrene au Musée de Valence* (exh. cat., Musée de Valence, Valence, 1985), pp. 102–03.

3 On Ango see: Sarah Boyer, 'Quelques propositions autour de Jean-Robert Ango (?–après le 16 janvier 1773),' *Les Cahiers de l'histoire de l'art*, 6 (2008), pp. 88–103.

4 Four further drawings executed with the same technique by Robert and Ango are known; cf. Sarah Catala, 'Les usages de la contre-épreuve dans le dessin français au XVIIIe siècle', *Les cahiers d'histoire de l'art*, 13 (2015), 35–43 (p. 41); Victor Carlson, 'Hubert Robert in Rome: Some Pen-and-Wash Drawings', *Master Drawings*, 39 (2001), 288–99 (p. 292).

5 Carlson (2001, p. 294) argues that these sheets provide evidence of a working relationship between Robert and Ango. For a recent discussion see S. Catala in Guillaume Faroult, et al., *Hubert Robert, 1733–1808: un peintre visionnaire* (exh. cat., Musée du Louvre, Paris, 2016), pp. 146–47, no. 13.

Cat. 7

1 See Christian Nebehay, *Egon Schiele: Sketch Books* (London: Thames and Hudson, 1989), pp. 180–81, figs. 132–33.

2 Leopold Museum, Vienna, inv. no. 2360; Kallir, p. 566, no. 1871; *Egon Schiele* (exh. cat., Albertina, Vienna, 2017), p. 330, no. 140.

3 Provenance listed in Jane Kallir, *Egon Schiele: The Complete Works* (New York: Harry N. Abrams, Inc., Publishers, 1990), p. 566, no. 1870.

Cat. 8

1 See Pierre Descargues, *Perspective*, ed. by Ellyn Childs Allison (New York: H. N. Abrams, 1977). For a 19th-century example see for instance Armand Cassagne, *Traité pratique de perspective appliquée au dessin artistique et industriel... Nouvelle édition revue et augmentée* (Paris: Librairie Classique Internationale A. Fouraut, 1889).

Cat. 9

1 Horst Janssen, *Minusio* (Frankfurt: Propylaen, 1973), n.p.

2 Riccardo Carazzetti, ed., *Remo Rossi: Antologica (1909–1982)* (exh. cat., Fondazione Remo Rossi, Locarno, 2012), p. 298.

3 Carazzetti, p. 44.

Cat. 10

1 For other American self-portraits by Grosz, see Mary Kay Flavell, *George Grosz: A Biography* (New Haven & London: Yale University Press, 1988), pp. 197–202.

2 Juerg M. Judin, ed., *George Grosz: The Years in America 1933–1958* (exh. cat., Nolan Judin, Berlin, 2009), pp. 176–77, no. 63.

Cat. 11

1 Anne L. Poulet, *Jean-Antoine Houdon: Sculptor of the Enlightenment* (exh. cat., National Gallery of Art, Washington, D.C, 2003), pp. 63–66, no. 1.

2 The same internal wooden frame is visible in Heinrich von Rustige's painting *The farmer in the artist's studio*, c. 1839, in the Stiftung Sammlung Volmer, Wuppertal; cf. Jane Munro, *Silent Partners: Artist and Mannequin from Function to Fetish* (exh. cat., Fitzwilliam Museum, Cambridge, 2014), p. 97, fig. 105.

3 See *Ermenegildo Antonio Donadini: Fotografie im königlichen Dresden 1881 bis 1914*, ed. by Jens Bove (Dresden: Edition Sächsische Zeitung SAXO'Phon, 2010).

Cat. 12

1 Royal Museums of Fine Arts of Belgium, Brussels; Anna Swinbourne, *James Ensor* (exh. cat., The Museum of Modern Art, New York, 2009), p. 52, plate 6; Xavier Tricot, *James Ensor. The Complete Paintings* (Ostfildern: Hatje Cantz, 2009), no. 166.

2 Herwig Todts, *James Ensor. Paintings and Drawings from the Collection of the Royal Museum of Fine Arts in Antwerp* (Schoten: BAI, 2008), see for instance p. 92 (*Self-portrait and sketch of a lamp*), and p. 117 (*Two masks*).

Cat. 13

1 See for instance his gouache, *Bricklayers on a building site*, 1875, private collection, New York; Michael Fried, *Menzel's Realism: Art and Embodiment in Nineteenth-Century Berlin* (New Haven and London: Yale University Press, 2002), pp. 157–59, fig. 104.

2 Fried, p. 219.

3 Georg Schäfer collection, Euerbach; Claude Kleisch and Marie Ursula Riemann-Reyher, eds., *Menzel (1815–1905), 'La névrose du vrai'* (exh. cat., Musée d'Orsay, Paris, 1996), p. 156 (ill. p. 155).

Cat. 14

1 Edmond and Jules de Goncourt, *Renée Mauperin* (Paris: G. Charpentier, 1890), p. 8.

2 Goncourt, p. 48.

3 Elisabeth Launay, *Les frères Goncourt collectionneurs de dessins* (Paris: Arthena, 1991), p. 57.

Cat. 15

1 Hans Naef, *Die Bildniszeichnungen von J.-A.-D. Ingres*, 5 vols. (Bern: Benteli Verlag, 1977-80), V (1980), pp. 74–77, nos. 289–90.

2 *Inventaire du Fonds Français: Bibliothèque Nationale, Département des Estampes*, (Paris: Bibliothèque Nationale, 1930), no. 37.

3 For Boucher-Desnoyers's stamp see Frits Lugt, *Les Marques de Collections de Dessins & d'Estampes*, no. 2789, online version; cf. Boucher-Desnoyers after Ingres, *Cameo depicting bust portraits of Ptolemy II and Arsinoe*, c. 1804, engraving, British Museum, inv. no. 1868,0822.955 (*Inventaire du Fonds Français*, no. 13).

Cat. 17

1 See Horst Uhr, *Lovis Corinth* (Berkeley, Los Angeles & Oxford: University of California Press, 1990), pp. 193ff.

2 See for instance: Uhr, pp. 260–61, figs. 166–68.

Cat. 18

1 Ariane James-Sarazin, with the collaboration of Jean-Yves Sarazin, *Hyacinthe Rigaud, 1659–1743* (Dijon: Éditions Faton, 2016), p. 595, no. D.16.

2 On this topic see Johannes Hartau, *Don Quijote in der Kunst. Wandlungen einer Symbolfigur* (Berlin: Mann, 1987), esp. pp. 232–33, figs. 194–95.

3 Cf. Claudia Breitkopf-Weinmann, et al., *Egon Schiele – Horst Janssen: Selbstinszenierung, Eros und Tod* (exh. cat., Leopold Museum, Vienna, 2004), pp. 106, 138, nos. 7, 36.

Cat. 19

1 Adelheid M. Gealt and Marcia E. Vetrocq, *Domenico Tiepolo's Punchinello Drawings* (exh. cat., Indiana University Art Museum, Bloomington, 1979), p. 92.

2 See Antonio Morassi, *A Complete Catalogue of the Paintings of G. B. Tiepolo* (London: Phaidon, 1962), p. 38, fig. 284.

Cat. 20

1 Discussed in: Alexandre Ananoff, *L'Oeuvre dessiné de Jean-Honoré Fragonard (1732–1806): catalogue raisonné*, 4 vols. (Paris: De Nobele, 1961–71), I (1961), no. 454, fig. 155; Pierre Rosenberg, *Fragonard* (exh. cat., Galeries Nationales du Grand Palais, Paris, 1987), under no. 255, fig. 1; Stein, *Fragonard: Drawing Triumphant*, under no. 79, note 5; Perrin Stein, 'The Dream of Fragonard', in *The Metropolitan Museum Blog*, 17 October 2016, <https://www.metmuseum.org/blogs/now-at-the-met/2016/fragonard-drawing-triumphant-dream-of-fragonard> [accessed 26 February 2018]; David Rand, 'Review: Fragonard, New York', *The Burlington Magazine*, 159 (2017), 166–67 (p. 166).

2 See Alain Guillerm, 'Les illustrations de Fragonard pour les Contes de La Fontaine', *Gazette des Beaux-Arts*, 89 (1977), pp. 99–105.

3 See Ananoff, I (1961), nos. 452, 455, II (1963), no. 987; Marianne Roland Michel, 'The Themes of "The Artist" and of "Inspiration" as revealed by some of Fragonard's Drawings', *The Burlington Magazine*, 103 (1961), pp. i-iii.

4 Mark P. McDonald, *Renaissance to Goya: Prints and Drawings from Spain* (exh. cat., The British Museum, London, 2012), p. 242, fig. 12.

Cat. 21

1 Arthur M. Hind, *Catalogue of Dutch and Flemish Drawings preserved in the Department of Prints and Drawings in the British Museum*, 4 vols. (London: British Museum Press, 1915–32), III (1915), no. 25.

2 Rijksmuseum, Amsterdam, inv. no. SK-A-298; Ruud Priem, et al., *Vermeer, Rembrandt and the Golden Age of Dutch Art: Masterpieces from the Rijksmuseum* (exh. cat., Vancouver Art Gallery, Vancouver, 2009), p. 42.

3 Rijksmuseum, Amsterdam, inv. no. RP-T-00-175; Priem, p. 43.

Cat. 22

1 Jules-Ernest Gérock, 'Un artiste strasbourgeois du XVIe siècle. David Kandel', *Archives alsaciennes d'histoire de l'art*, 2 (1923), 84–96 (pp. 86–90).

2 Musée du Louvre, Cabinet des Dessins, Paris, inv. no. 18708.

3 Musée du Louvre, Cabinet des Dessins, Paris, inv. no. 18707; Ewa Letkiewicz, '"L' Orphelin", un portrait de Nicolas Christophe Radziwiłł par David Kandel identifié dans les collections du Louvre', *La revue des musées de France*, 60 (2010), 1, pp. 48–52, 109, 111; Karl Theodore Parker, *Alsatian Drawings of the XV and XVI Century* (London: P. & D. Colnaghi & Co., Publishers, 1928), p. 34, no. 60.

SELECT BIBLIOGRAPHY

Aymonino, Adriano, and Lauder, Anne Varick, *Drawn from the Antique: Artists & the Classical Ideal* (exh. cat., Sir John Soane's Museum, London, 2015)

Bacci, Michele, *Il Pennello dell'Evangelista: Storia delle Immagini Sacre Attribuite a San Luca* (Pisa: GISEM Edizioni ETS, 1998)

Bermingham, Ann, *Learning to Draw: Studies in the Cultural History of a Polite and Useful Art* (New Haven and London: Yale University Press, 2000)

Emison, Patricia A., *Creating the 'Divine' Artist from Dante to Michelangelo* (Leiden and Boston: Brill, 2004)

Faroult, Guillaume, et al., *Hubert Robert, 1733–1808: un peintre visionnaire* (exh. cat., Musée du Louvre, Paris, 2016)

Filipczak, Zirka Zaremba, *Picturing Art in Antwerp 1550–1700* (Princeton, NJ: Princeton University Press, 1987)

Fried, Michael, *Menzel's Realism: Art and Embodiment in Nineteenth-Century Berlin* (New Haven and London: Yale University Press, 2002)

Gealt, Adelheid M. and Vetrocq, Marcia E., *Domenico Tiepolo's Punchinello Drawings* (exh. cat., Indiana University Art Museum, Bloomington, 1979)

Goethe, Johann Wolfgang von, *Italian Journey (1786–1788)*, trans. by W. H. Auden and Elizabeth Mayer (Harmondsworth: Penguin Books, 1970)

Goffen, Rona, *Renaissance Rivals: Michelangelo, Leonardo, Raphael, Titian* (New Haven and London: Yale University Press, 2004)

Kallir, Jane, *Egon Schiele: The Complete Works* (New York: Harry N. Abrams, Inc., Publishers, 1990)

Koerner, Joseph Leo, *Caspar David Friedrich and the Subject of Landscape* (London: Reaktion, 1990)

Mariani, Giordana Canova, et al., *Luca Evangelista: Parola e Immagine tra Oriente e Occidente* (exh. cat., Diocesan Museum, Padua, 2000)

McHam, Sarah Blacke, *Pliny and the Artistic Culture of the Italian Renaissance: The Legacy of the Natural History* (New Haven and London: Yale University Press, 2013)

Munro, Jane, *Silent Partners: Artist and Mannequin from Function to Fetish* (exh. cat., Fitzwilliam Museum, Cambridge, 2015)

Petherbridge, Deanna, *The Primacy of Drawing; Histories and Theories of Practice* (New Haven and London: Yale University Press, 2010)

Pliny, *Natural History Books XXXIII–XXXV* (Loeb Classical Library), trans. by H. Rackham (Cambridge, MA and London: Harvard University Press, 1999)

Schulz, Wolfgang, 'Doomer and Savery', *Master Drawings*, 9 (1971), pp. 253–59, 316–31

Sloan, Kim, *'A Noble Art': Amateur Artists and Drawing Masters c. 1600–1800* (exh. cat., The British Museum, London, 2000)

Stein, Perrin, et al., *Fragonard: Drawing Triumphant. Works from New York Collections* (exh. cat., The Metropolitan Museum of Art, New York, 2016)

Todts, Herwig, *James Ensor. Paintings and Drawings from the Collection of the Royal Museum of Fine Arts in Antwerp* (Schoten: BAI, 2008)

Uhr, Horst, *Lovis Corinth* (Berkeley, Los Angeles & Oxford: University of California Press, 1990)

PHOTOGRAPHIC CREDITS

All images © Matthew Hollow, except: figs. 2, 5, 14, 21, cat. 21 © The Trustees of the British Museum; fig. 3 ©Photographic Archive Museo Nacional del Prado; fig. 6 By permission of the Governing Body of Christ Church, Oxford; cat. 1 © The Samuel Courtauld Trust, The Courtauld Gallery, London; cat. 9, 12, 18 © DACS 2018; fig. 16 Fondazione Remo Rossi Locarno © Roberto Pellegrini; cat. 10, fig. 17 © Estate of George Grosz, Princeton, N.J. / DACS 2018; fig. 18 SLUB Dresden / Deutsche Fotothek / Ermenegildo Antonio Donadini; fig. 19 © Rheinisches Bildarchiv, rba_c004709; fig. 20 Digital image courtesy of the Getty's Open Content Program